Fifty Favourite Dry Flies

T. Donald Overfield

Fifty Favourite Dry Flies

with illustrations by the author,
and colour photographs by John Goddard

Ernest Benn Limited
London & Tonbridge

Published by
Ernest Benn Limited
25 New Street Square, London EC4A 3JA
& Sovereign Way, Tonbridge, Kent TN9 1RW

First published 1980
©T. Donald Overfield 1980
ISBN 0 510-22526-8

Typeset by Reproduction Drawings Ltd, Sutton, Surrey
Printed in Great Britain
by W. & J. Mackay Limited, Chatham

British Library Cataloguing in Publication Data
Overfield, Thomas Donald
    Fifty favourite dry flies.
    1. Fly tying 2. Trout fishing
    I. Title II. Goddard, John
    688.7'9   SH451

    ISBN 0 510-22526-8

Contents

Contents

Foreword

The reception you gave to *Fifty Favourite Nymphs,* the first in the "Fifty Favourite" series, has prompted me to take up brush and pen and launch myself into *Fifty Favourite Dry Flies,* hoping that within these pages you will discover some patterns that, after due trial, will become your own favourite trout takers.

The history of the dry fly is not long in terms of angling history. The wet fly commanded the stage for centuries, and while I am convinced that many thoughtful fly fishers did experiment with various floating flies, their dressings, with one or two exceptions, slipped through the net of recorded history, leaving the major noted advances in the dry fly field to the era when the eyed hook was invented and the Golden Age of the chalk streams began.

It is true that G.E.M. Skues made waves in the dry fly pool when his nymphs disturbed that smooth surface, bringing a measure of sanity back to the southern streams. We should never denigrate the original research of the early experimenters, however, for the well designed floating fly has a sure place in the armoury of the angler, witnessed by the flies in this book.

My method of tying in the hackle may cause a few raised eyebrows. When tying for exhibition or competition purposes, where the only criteria is to provide a dressing that will please man, then I do tie in the hackle during the early stages of the fly's construction, for without doubt a fly tied so presents a more pleasing, and neat, aspect. However, the trout cares not one jot or tittle when the hackle is secured, in the same way that he does not shy away from a pattern that boasts ten whisks when the natural has only two or three. I do know that my blood pressure rises rapidly if having spent time and effort in completing the body, whisks, rib, wings, etc., only to find that the hackle is a rogue, refusing to wind in the approved manner, or worse, breaks off. I lay down no dogmatic rules about it and the choice is yours. Unkind friends have suggested that I show the hackle tied in last to avoid having to illustrate a hackle time after time. Not true!

But now to the tying vice. I am confident that after a fair trial you will find at least some of these fifty patterns will become your own favourites. They are all proven dry flies, having fooled countless trout of chalkstream, burn and still-water. Good luck!

T. Donald Overfield
Solihull, Warwickshire, 1979

Colour Plates

The colour plates in this section are of considerable interest, for in many instances the flies shown were actually tied by their inventors; I would particularly draw to your attention the Little Marryat (Marryat: 1840 – 1896) and the Quill Gordon (Gordon: 1854 – 1915), two very historic patterns from my collection. Where it was not possible to obtain flies from the originators then replicas have been tied especially for this book by James Nice of Sidmouth. Full details appear in the following table.

Pattern	Originator	Illustrated fly tied by
1 Hawthorn	Jacobsen	Jacobsen
2 Rough Olive	Woolley	Nice
3 Sanctuary	Sanctuary	Nice
4 Dogsbody	Powell	Nice
5 Little Red Sedge	Skues	Nice
6 Imperial	Kite	Kite
7 Ogden's Cockwing	Ogden	Nice
8 Red Tag	Flynn	Nice
9 Greenwell's Glory	Greenwell/Wright	Nice
10 Devon Constable	Nice	Nice
11 John Storey	Storey	Storey
12 Jacques' Mayfly	Jacques	Nice
13 Beacon Beige	Deane	Deane
14 Little Marryat	Marryat	Marryat
15 Lunn's Particular	Lunn	Nice
16 Yellow May Dun	Price	Price
17 Quill Gordon	Gordon	Gordon
18 Goddard Caddis	Goddard	Goddard
19 Golden Eyed Gauze Wing	Price	Price
20 Royal Coachman	Haily	Nice
21 Pale Watery	R. Walker	Walker
22 Grey Wulff	Deane	Deane
23 Iron Blue Dun	unknown	Nice
24 Daddy Longlegs	R. Walker	Walker
25 Polymay	R. Walker	Walker
26 Last Hope	Goddard	Goddard
27 Kahl Sedge	Kahl	Kahl
28 Grayling Fiddler	Horsfall Turner	Horsfall Turner
29 Grey Duster	unknown	Nice
30 No Hackle	Swisher	Swisher
31 Blue Winged Olive	C. F. Walker	Nice
32 Pope's Nondescript	Pope	Nice
33 Wake Fly Sedge	Price	Price

Pattern	Originator	Illustrated fly tied by
34 Misty Blue Dun	Waites	Waites
35 Kai-Fly	Pitt	Pitt
36 Ridsdale's Favourite	Ridsdale	Nice
37 Little Claret Spinner	Jacobsen	Jacobsen
38 Grey Fox Variant	Flick	Flick
39 Super Grizzly	Goddard	Goddard
40 Barton Bug	Darlington	Darlington
41 Terry's Terror	Deane	Deane
42 Assassine	Pequegnot	Pequegnot
43 Devon Dumpling	Nice	Nice
44 Driffield Dun	unknown	Nice
45 Tup's Indispensable	Austin	Nice
46 Itchen Olive	Mackie	Mackie
47 Wickham's Fancy	Wickham	Nice
48 Mistigri	Pequegnot	Pequegnot
49 Hassam's Pet	Hassam	Nice
50 Merry Widow	Elphick	Elphick

1 Hawthorn

2 Rough Olive

3 Sanctuary 4 Dogsbody

5 Little Red Sedge 6 Imperial

7 Ogden's Cockwing 8 Red Tag

9 Greenwell's Glory 10 Devon Constable

11 John Storey

12 Jacques' Mayfly

13 Beacon Beige

14 Little Marryat

15 Lunn's Particular

16 Yellow May Dun

17 Quill Gordon

18 Goddard Caddis

19 Golden Eyed Gauze Wing

20 Royal Coachman

21 Pale Watery

22 Grey Wulff

23 Iron Blue Dun

24 Daddy Longlegs

25 Polymay

26 Last Hope

13

27 Kahl Sedge

28 Grayling Fiddler

29 Grey Duster

30 No Hackle

31 Blue Winged Olive

32 Pope's Nondescript

33 Wake Fly Sedge

34 Misty Blue Dun

35 Kai-Fly

36 Ridsdale's Favourite

37 Little Claret Spinner

38 Grey Fox Variant

39 Super Grizzly

40 Barton Bug

41 Terry's Terror

42 Assassine

43 Devon Dumpling

44 Driffield Dun

45 Tup's Indispensable

46 Itchen Olive

47 Wickham's Fancy

48 Mistigri

49 Hassam's Pet

50 Merry Widow

Fifty Favourite Dry Flies

Hawthorn Fly

Jacobsen

It is a great pleasure for me to start off this book with a fly that has its origins in Scandinavia. We British fly fishers tend to imagine that angling stops where the seas begin, or to stretch the boundaries somewhat, into Ireland. We ignore the great development work in fly design carried out beyond our shores. Such countries as Denmark, Norway, America, France and Spain come to mind where progressive fly design work is constantly going on. In this book you will find designs from some of those countries. However, we are concentrating on a pattern of the Hawthorn fly, *Bibio marci*, devised by my old fishing companion Preben Torp Jacobsen, possibly the best fly tyer in Denmark. His profession, that of a vet, gives him a head start over other tyers in the collecting of materials!

It has been my pleasure to fish with Preben. He is not an unknown visitor to these shores, where he has many friends. I shall long remember the flood of laughter that came from the "Black Dane" when he cast most carefully into my local water, the Blyth, to a minute rise form and hooked a very small minnow on a No. 20 Black Gnat. Such valiant fishing called for a drink—with Preben every fish calls for a drink—and he produced from a flask that seemed forever full a strange concoction, brewed midst the snows, that had the kick of a demented mule. After the

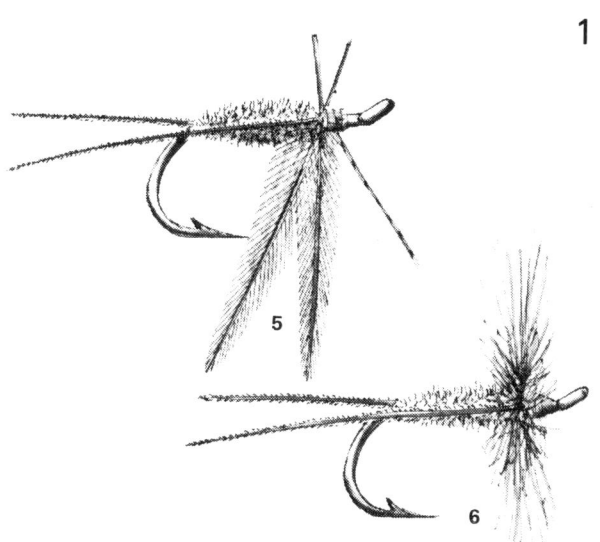

5

6

second drink my interest in fishing waned considerably.

But enough of the anecdotal side, and to the fly-tying bench. The Hawthorn fly has long been mentioned in fly-fishing literature, but few anglers set much store by it. I suspect it is because the natural fly has such a short season and the angler is not on the water when it appears. Most knowledgable angling entomologists, and I am not one of them, assert that the fly appears on the water towards the end of April and has but a short season, some two or three weeks. When the fly is on the water, however, the trout go mad. This opinion I can confirm, because a location I fish sees these insects for but a few days, but when they are about I have had capital sport, and I would not like to be without a dressing of this fly. My choice is Jacobsen's.

Place in the vice a hook between number 10 and 12 and wind down the shank the brown waxed silk, 1, continuing to the bend where you tie in three black condor herls, 2. Twist the condor herls together around the tying silk and wind on a well-tapered body, 3. Now tie in two black condor herl tips, well splayed out and pointing to the rear, 4. Remove the waste ends and tie in two black cock hackles, back to back, 5. Wind together to form a dense, tightly packed, hackle, 6, completing the fly with a well varnished whip finish.

Rough Olive

Woolley

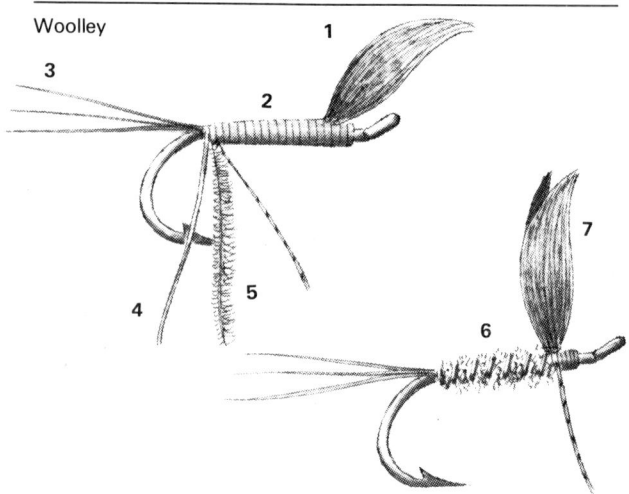

Roger Woolley was a highly competent professional fly tyer who built up a regular clientele at the turn of the century and later. Born in 1877 at Tutbury, Derbyshire, he came to know extremely well the streams that Izaak Walton fished those long years ago: the Dove, the Manifold, the Derbyshire Derwent and the Blythe. He extended his fly-tying knowledge when in 1896 he took employment as a coachman in Ireland to a member of the gentry. His two years in that country were days of work and nights of fishing and fly tying, and his investigations into fly tying at that time brought him to the craftsman's peak. Obviously he had a mentor, but history does not relate the man's name, alas.

In 1888 Woolley had the confidence to return to Derbyshire, to Hatton, where he started the dual career of fly tyer and hairdresser . . . strange how many good fly tyers were hairdressers. Like all top-line fly dressers, Woolley relied upon his observation of the natural insect rather than follow the written-down patterns of others. His reputation grew apace and soon anglers were demanding Woolley flies. His hairdressing took something of a back seat. He received the ultimate accolade when G.E.M. Skues wrote in his *Nymph Fishing for Chalk Stream Trout* "tackle dealers in general, wholesale or retail, with few exceptions . . . of

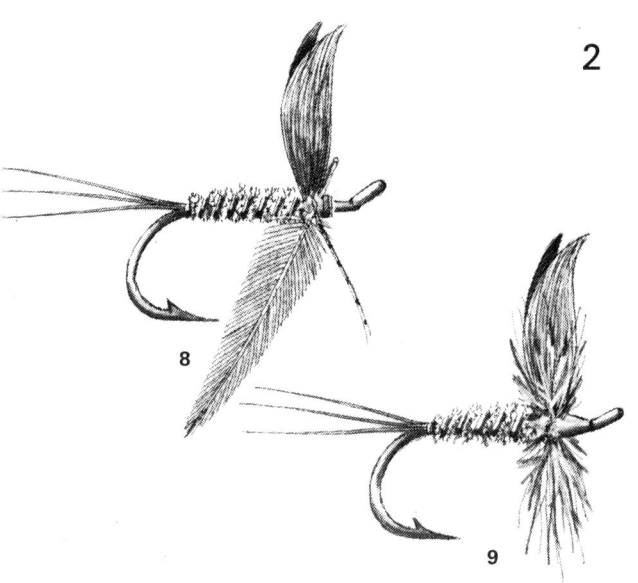

8

9

whom Mr. Roger Woolley of Hatton, Derbyshire and Mr. T. J. Hanna of Stanard Street, Moneymore, Co. Derry, are bright examples . . . make little effort at genuine representation''.

'In 1932 the articles Woolley had written for the now defunct *Fishing Gazette* were published in book form as *Modern Trout Fly Dressings*, a most informative book that covered many styles and now commands a high price in the book dealers' lists. In 1938 he published *Fly Fishers' Flies*, a useful beginners' guide to streamside entomology and the matching artificials they should use.

Woolley was blessed with a long and active life, dying in 1959 at the age of 82 within casting distance of his beloved Derbyshire streams. His memory is continued for me in his version of the Rough Olive.

Place in the vice a number 14 hook. Start down the shank a length of dark green tying silk and tie in two slips of dark starling or hen blackbird feather fibre, 1. Continue the silk to the bend, 2, and tie in dark olive cock hackle fibres, 3, followed by a length of gold wire, 4, and a length of olive dyed heron herl, 5. Complete the body, 6, and bring the wings into an upright position, 7. Tie in a dark olive cock hackle, 8, and complete the fly with a neatly varnished whip finished head.

The Sanctuary

Sanctuary

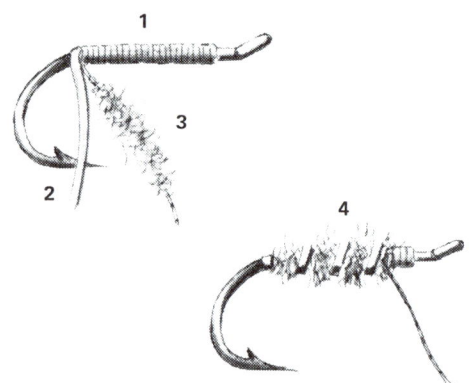

I have always had a close affection for this particular pattern, on two counts: one, that I have had the pleasure of fishing the southern chalk streams that Dr. Thomas Sanctuary knew well in his hey-day, and secondly, I am now a member of the Pickering Fisheries Association which controls, along with other waters, the northern chalk stream known as the Costa, one of the doctor's favourite waters in the latter years of his life when he was living at Scarborough.

Dr. Sanctuary was born in the year 1844 in the south of the country and educated in that famous school, Winchester, that produced quite a number of great fly fishers. The college was situated near the banks of the Itchen where many a tyro first wet a fly. One of Sanctuary's great companions was George Selwyn Marryat, the man who taught F. M. Halford to tie flies and whose presence is evident in Halford's written works. Sanctuary had many friends in that Golden Era of the dry fly, one being H. S. Hall, the man who perfected the eyed hook and gave added impetus to the dry fly movement. He was also friendly with the famed fly tyer George Holland of Salisbury, (and later of Winchester), who operated from the year 1885. In fact it was Sanctuary and Hall who first showed Holland how to tie trout flies. The good doctor was certainly in the midst of the dry fly revolution at the turn of the century.

Sanctuary's middle years are somewhat shrouded in

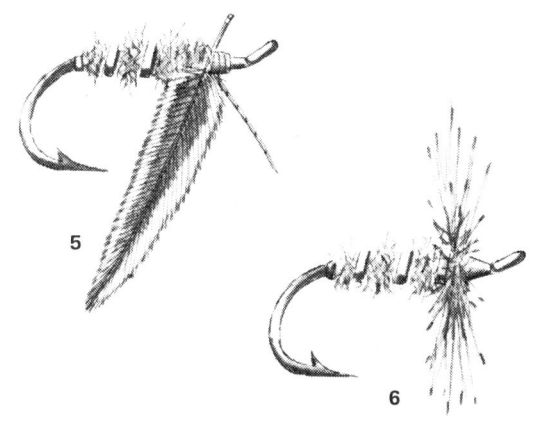

mystery. We have reason to suppose that he moved from the south to the Midlands; unconfirmed reports indicate that he settled in the Redditch area of Worcestershire, before moving north to live at Scarborough. The years of these two moves are not known to me and I would welcome any information about this eminent dry fly angler.

When Sanctuary died on 4 April 1931 a contemporary wrote: "Last season, though growing feeble, he still had occasional days on the Costa and the Pickering Beck. Unable to move far he could still manage to get a brace and a half or so. When he found his fish on the move he would sit over it until he got it, and never once did the fish suspect his presence. Less than six months ago he spent hours tying exquisite flies".

Dr. Sanctuary was buried on 8 April 1931, at Kirby Misperton, almost within sight of the streams he loved so much in his closing years. I have long considered this one of my favourite patterns and welcome the chance to present it to a wider audience.

Place a number 14 hook in the vice. Take the brown tying silk, 1, down the shank. Tie in a length of flat gold tinsel, 2, and then dub the silk with dark hare's ear fur, 3. Complete the body and rib same, 4. Tie in a coch-y-bondhu cock hackle, 5, and wind in close even turns, 6. Complete the fly with a whip-finished head.

Dogsbody

Powell

This dry fly must surely be one of the most effective patterns used today. Devised by the late Harry Powell it was born in the year 1924 when he was in business as a barber and hairdresser . . . another man who snipped the locks for a living, like Roger Woolley . . . at the well-known Welsh angling venue of Usk. Powell had an assistant, William Hickey, who fortunately recorded the birth of the Dogsbody.

It seems that one afternoon Powell and Hickey were tying up flies for a mail-order customer. Their model was an example that had been sent to them. Try as they would they could not match the exact texture and colour of the sample's body. No doubt they were near to desperation when into the shop came a farmer and his dog, the latter being described by Hickey as a rather "foxy looking animal". They both realised that some of the hairs on the dog were just what they were seeking and so while Hickey snipped away at the farmer Powell gave the dog a modest trim. When the farmer and his dog had departed Powell and his assistant turned once more to fly tying. Combing out the downy hairs at the base they found the ideal colour and texture to match the sample. As the fly at that time had no name they christened it the Dogsbody.

Down the years it has become a firm favourite of many

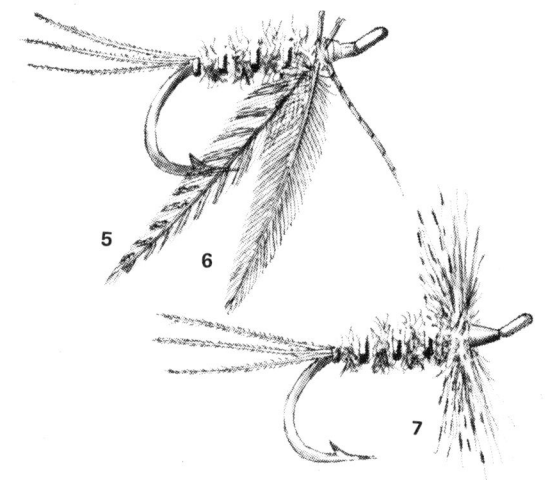

fly fishers, myself included. Courtney Williams considered that it killed best from April until mid June, and again in September. Personally I have found it to be equally effective all through the season as a general purpose fly. I put it in the same catagory as Kite's Imperial. Strangely I do not find it a good grayling fly though Hickey thought it to be so. Perhaps my East Yorkshire grayling have differing tastes than the Welsh variety.

The tying is quite straight forward, but to describe the true colour of the dog hair is not easy. I suppose the best description is a sandy camel colour, as found in some pale Labradors, the soft under-hair being what I prefer.

The hook is usually 14 or 16. The brown tying silk, 1, is taken in close even turns down to the bend. There tie in three strands of cock pheasant tail fibres as the whisks, 2, followed by a length of oval gold tinsel, 3. Now wax the tying silk and dub it with the aformentioned dog's hair, 4. Wind on the dubbed silk to form the body and rib with open turns of the oval gold tinsel. Now tie in a Plymouth Rock cock hackle, 5, and a dark red cock hackle, 6. The original pattern has the Plymouth rock wound on first, followed by the dark-red cock as shown in figure 7. Personally I always wind them together. The choice is yours. Complete with a whip finished head.

Little Red Sedge

Skues

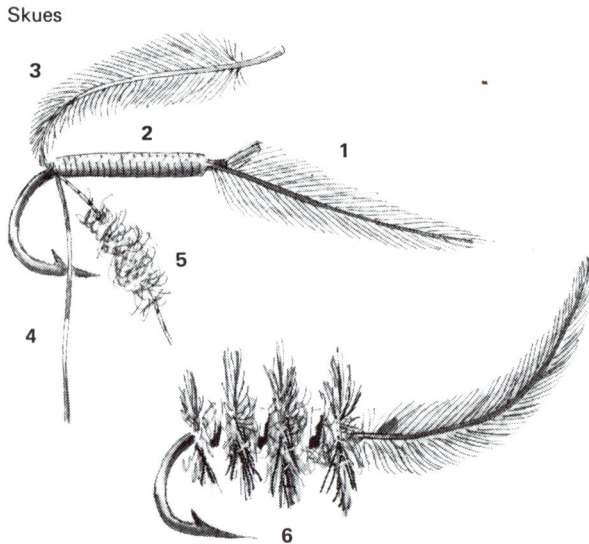

This excellent dry sedge pattern came from the vice of
G. E. M. Skues (1858 – 1949). In his lifetime he had a pro-
found effect on fly fishing, and in particular the development of nymph representation and nymph fishing. Because
he is so well known for his impact on upstream nymphing,
some people think he did not approve of dry fly work. This
is certainly not so, for his many books show a very clear ap-
preciation of the use of the dry fly.

His Little Red Sedge is a cracking pattern for those calm
late evenings of summer when, as night falls, the larger
trout come forth from their bankside holts to take the scut-
tering sedges. Skues called the fly a "nailer", a most
descriptive word, and he considered it ideal for when the
trout are nosing about on the weed and near the surface.
He firmly believed that if you presented the fly close by
such a hunting trout you would be sure to get him.
Stillwater anglers who know well the weed beds of the
margins will know if Skues was right.

The pattern also has a good reputation as a grayling
killer. Certainly Skues caught countless numbers of these
fine winter fish on his Abbots Barton beats of the Itchen
but, like the Dogsbody, I have not found it to be the liking

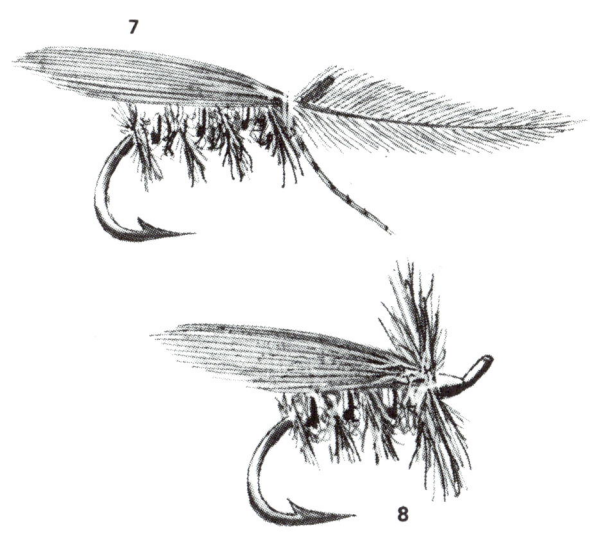

of my Yorkshire grayling. Nevertheless, I would never venture on the stream when after the trout without a few Little Red Sedges in my fly box.

I have taken certain liberties with Skues' original dressing for the simple reason that materials that were common in his day are now extremely rare; for example, he calls for landrail (corncrake) wings and so I have substituted dyed hen wing fibres.

Take the required hook and after starting the tying silk of hot orange waxed with brown wax down the shank tie in a natural deep red cock hackle, 1. Continue the silk down the shank, 2, and at the bend tie in another cock hackle of the same colour, 3, followed by a length of fine gold wire, 4. Now dub the tying silk with darkest hare's ear fur, 5.

Wind the dubbed silk up the body, and then wind the body hackle, followed by the ribbing to secure it, 6. Secure all and remove the waste. Tie in a piece of light brown hen wing feather fibre, bunched and rolled, to make the wing, 7. Now wind five or six turns of the head hackle over the wing root, 8, and complete this excellent sedge pattern with a neatly whipped head.

Kite's Imperial

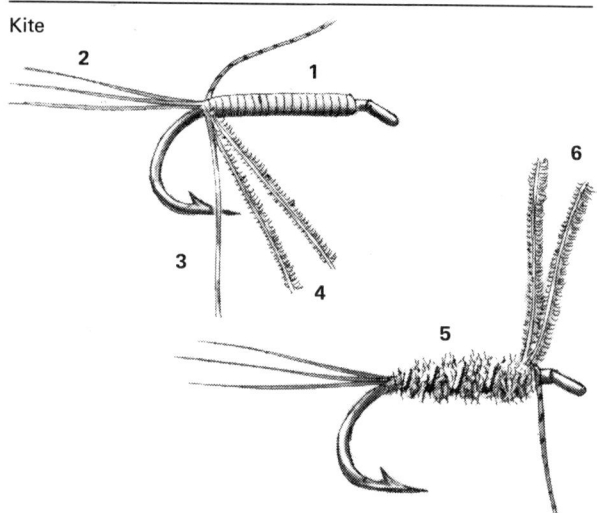

Kite

I had the distinct pleasure of knowing the originator of this pattern, and spent quite a few happy hours in his company. His death in June 1968 at the early age of 48 robbed the world of a highly perceptive author, skilled angler and a most thoughtful amateur entomologist, the latter being evident in his original fly-tying patterns. A career officer who left the army in 1965 and whose few remaining years were plagued with heart problems, he died on the banks of the Test one fine June morning.

His fly, the Kite's Imperial, was the outcome of a day's fishing on the River Teifi in Wales during the early part of the 1962 season. He collected from the water some specimens of the male large olive dun, translating into feather and herl what his amateur entomologists's eyes showed him. He described the pattern in his regular weekly column of *Shooting Times* and it very rapidly became a favourite of many fly fishers, myself included. I would go so far as to say that if I were to be restricted to but three flies, then Ollie's creation would be among them.

Though only 17 years old, the pattern is to be seen in tackle shops dressed with materials that bear no relationship to the original. I have seen it offered for sale with a peacock herl body, with a body of purple silk, with hackles

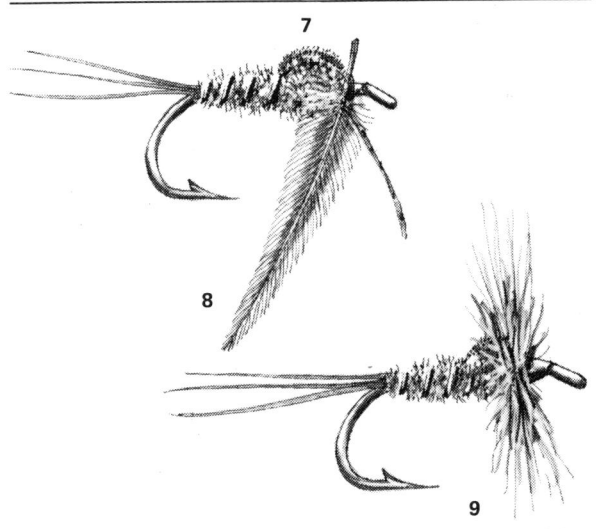

ranging from dark red to blue dun, and without tail whisks.
I wonder how accurate are the patterns of yesteryear if a fly
that is not so old can be thus bastardised. At least this book
gives me the chance to put the matter right so far as Kite's
fly is concerned.

The hook size should be number 14. Kite was not at all
fussy about up-eyed or down-eyed hooks. Nor, I suspect,
are the trout. The tying silk is purple, taken down the hook
shank, 1, and at the bend tie in a bunch of greyish-brown
cock hackle fibres, 2, if used in the spring. For the summer
the fibres should be honey-dun. Now tie in a length of fine
gold wire, 3, and undyed herls of the heron, 4.

Wind the herls together to form the body and rib in place
with the gold wire, 5. Secure and remove the waste wire,
leaving the ends of the herls, 6. Double and re-double the
herls to create the thorax hump, 7. Secure and snip off
waste. Tie in a honey-dun hackle of top quality, 8, or, if
that is unobtainable, a good light ginger will suffice.
Carefully wind in close even turns and secure, 9. Remove
waste and complete the fly with a neatly varnished whip
finish.

You may fish this pattern with absolute confidence
wherever rivers hold trout.

Ogden's Cockwing

Ogden

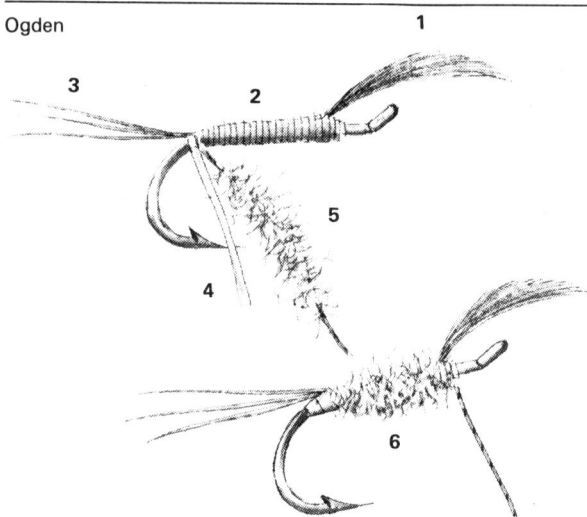

Some fly fishers fall into the trap of believing a pattern that was invented last year and took trout for some well known angler must be a much better fly than some old confection. I would disabuse them of such thoughts. Admittedly many old patterns are no better, or worse, than all the thousands of new patterns that enthusiastic amateur dressers "invent" every year, soon to be swept downstream into oblivion. But there is one old fly I have used for years and which is worth publicising. I refer to the fly known as Ogden's Fancy.

The purists amongst us may consider that the lack of a cock hackle should put it beyond the dry fly pale, but I do not share that view. With the application of the excellent modern floatants available, the fly floats supremely well.

The inventor of this particular Cockwing—there have been flies with the same name by other tyers—was James Ogden. Born in Matlock, Derbyshire, Ogden moved to Cheltenham, Gloucestershire, in early manhood and there set up as a tackle dealer and fly tyer. His fame as a fly tyer spread and it is of passing interest to note that he was the first man to set out clearly the tying of a dry fly. That is, I think, quite well established. In his book *Ogden on Fly Tying*, 1879, he indicates that he was tying dry flies "forty years ago". This would pre-date Pulman by a matter of two

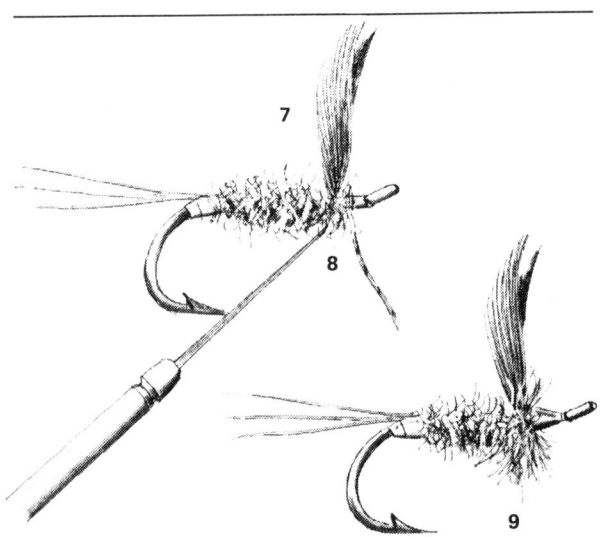

years or so. I am quite confident however that dry flies had been used for many a year but no-one had bothered to record the fact.

Another famous fly invented by James Ogden was the Invicta, which I hope to feature in a further volume *Fifty Favourite Wet Flies*. Folk lore has it that so effective was this pattern that on some waters it was actually banned!

But let us turn to the Cockwing, sometimes known as the Hare's Ear Blue Dun. The hook is generally a size 14. Having secured the hook in the vice and started the yellow tying silk down the shank, tie in two wing slips of starling fibre, 1, slightly tinged with yellow dye. Continue the silk down the hook shank, 2, and at the bend tie in red cock hackle fibres for the whisks, 3, followed by a length of gold tinsel, 4. Wind the tinsel round the shank and under the whisks to form a small collar and then dub the silk with fur from a hare's ear mixed with strands of olive wool fibre, 5. Wind the dubbed silk up the hook to form the body, 6, and bring the wings into an upright position, securing with turns of silk round the base, 7. Take further turns of the dubbed silk in front of the wings, remove waste and secure. With a dubbing needle tease out long strands for the legs, 8. Complete the fly with a whip finish, 9.

Red Tag

Flynn

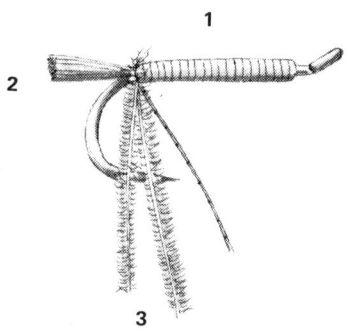

Now we come to a cracking fly that has a great reputation as a grayling taker. I had long considered the pattern to be of Yorkshire origin but it would seem that it may well have been invented further south, in Worcestershire, around the period 1850. Thought to have been invented by a man called Flynn who was a regular angler on the river Teme, it was originally called the Worcester Gem.

Some 25 years after it was devised, the northern author and angler F. M. Walbran was given a few examples and used them on his native rivers, the Yore and the Wharfe. The first time he used the fly, during the fence months and when he was after grayling, he records that he brought 25 fish to the net. Just where the name Red Tag comes from I have yet to discover, though I suspect the name was bestowed upon it by Walbran.

The angling historian Courtney Williams put forward the view that it was usually fished wet. I would certainly refute that statement, for most of the fly fishers of my acquaintance fish a dry fly version of the pattern. Williams also records that the original Worcester Gem had a tag made of

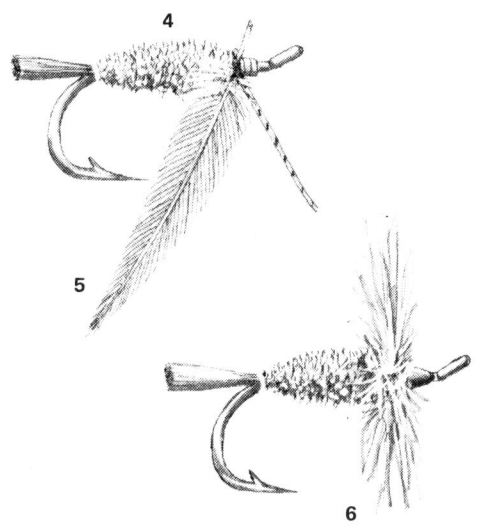

strands from a woodpecker's crest, also that a turn or two of gold or silver tinsel was wound under the tag. I have not been able to verify this.

I hasten to assure you that the Red Tag is not only good as a grayling fly. I have found it to be a capital trout taker in northern waters, and rainbow trout, where introduced into the streams, seem to find it most attractive, though strange to relate I have only found it to be super-effective in the first three months of the season.

To tie the fly is not at all difficult. Usually it is dressed on a number 14 hook, though I have had capital sport on a 16. Having secured the hook in the vice take the green tying silk down the hook shank in close even turns, 1, tying in a length of bright red wool, or if you have such a thing, a piece of scarlet ibis feather, 2. Having made that secure tie in strands of bright green peacock herl, ideally from the eye feather, 3. Twist the strands together and wind to form the body, 4. Now tie in a sharp bright natural red cock hackle, 5. Wind the hackle in close even turns, 6, and complete the fly with a neatly varnished whip finish.

Greenwell's Glory

Greenwell and Wright

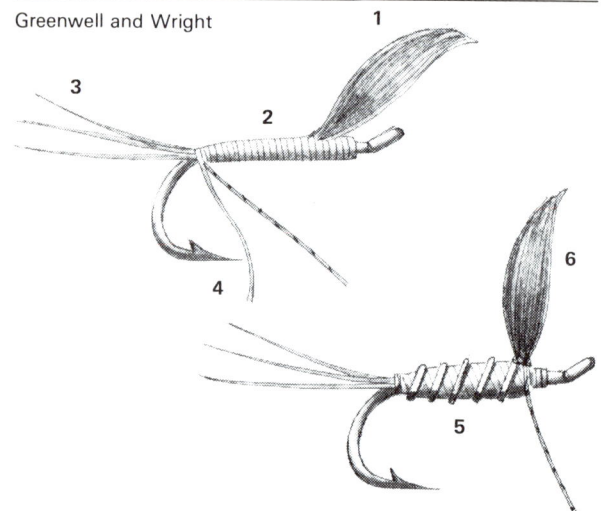

Ask a person who knows nothing about our chosen sport to name a trout fly and I would bet he would give you two: the Bloody Butcher and the Greenwell's Glory.

I am sure it is almost superfluous for me to give the history of this pattern, so well know is it, but for the newcomers to our craft I will do so; others must bear with me.

It was first tied by a famous Scottish fly dresser, James Wright, in May 1854. Wright lived at the village of Sprouston near to the River Tweed and it was to this area that a prelate of Durham Cathedral, one William Greenwell, came every year to fish. After a most frustrating day on the Tweed Greenwell arrived at Wright's door fishless, but bearing an example of the natural insect on which the trout had been so avidly feeding, having ignored the cleric's selection of artificials. He asked Wright to tie up some artificials to match the natural. This was done and the next day Greenwell had a basket of fish.

What was the natural fly? History does not tell us, but we can guess it was one of the olives. But the question remains, did old Wright pass off to the cleric a fly pattern that had long been known on the Tweed, a pattern devised by Mark Aitken and known only as Number VIII, for it is uncannily

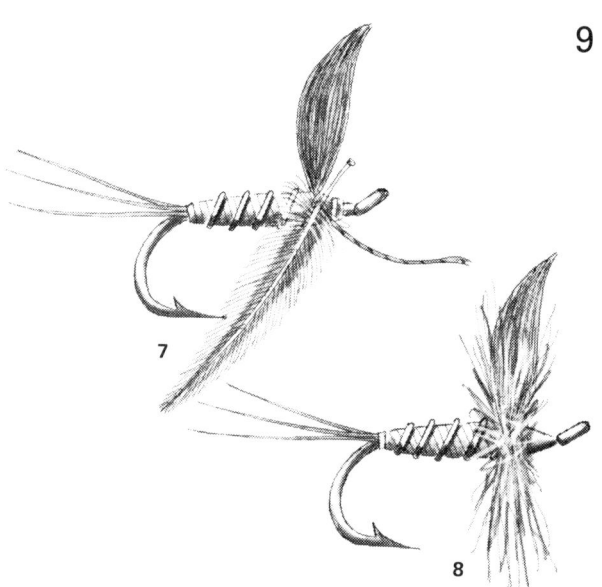

7

8

like the Greenwell's Glory? Space does not permit us to
delve deeper but those who are interested will find nine
pages devoted to Wright and his work in my book *Famous
Flies and Their Originators,* published in 1972.

Obviously the original pattern was a wet fly, but when
the dry fly came into its own thoughtful dressers took the
view that so successful a pattern may easily be converted to
a dry fly to represent quite a few of the olive duns. The
original pattern did not have tail whisks but contemporary
dressings have them as an aid to flotation.

The hook size is generally number 14. Start the tying silk,
yellow well-waxed with brown wax to give it a positive olive
hue, down the hook shank and tie in two slips of fibre from
the inside feather of a blackbird's wing, 1. Continue the silk
down the shank to the bend 2, and there tie in the light
ginger tail whisks, 3, followed by a length of fine gold wire,
4.

Wind the silk back up the shank in close even turns to
form the body and rib with close turns of the gold wire, 5.
Secure and remove waste ribbing. Take the tying silk round
the wing roots and bring to an upright position, 6. Tie in a
coch y bondu cock hackle, 7, and wind behind and in front
of the wings, 8. Complete with a varnished head.

Devon Constable

Nice

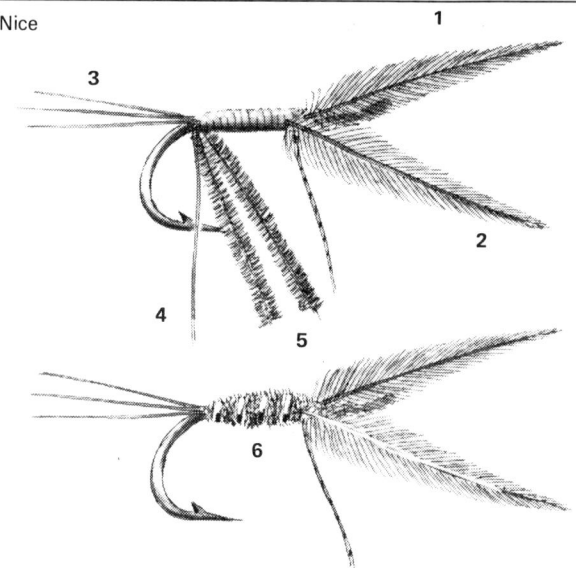

More years ago than I care to imagine I made the aquaintance of a man who, in my opinion, is quite possibly one of the top five fly tyers in Britain. His skills at the vice go hand in hand with a lifetime of experience fishing the streams and still waters of his native county of Devon. Consequently many of his patterns are brought about by observing the natural insects, though I hasten to add that this pattern had its origins elsewhere.

When I was planning my limited de luxe edition of *The Way of a Man with a Trout*, containing artificial nymphs dressed strictly to Skues' prescription, I had no hesitation in choosing Nice to do the work. Why? Because of his uncanny ability to reproduce the style of any fly tyer after due examination, coupled with incredible neatness. Many of the flies shown in the colour plates of this book have been tied by their originators and are so noted. All the other flies have been tied by Jim Nice.

Now to the Devon Constable, a highly thought of local pattern in Devon that goes back 40 years or so. Originally devised by a member of the police force who was based at Honiton, he passed the dressing on to Nice. My friend is

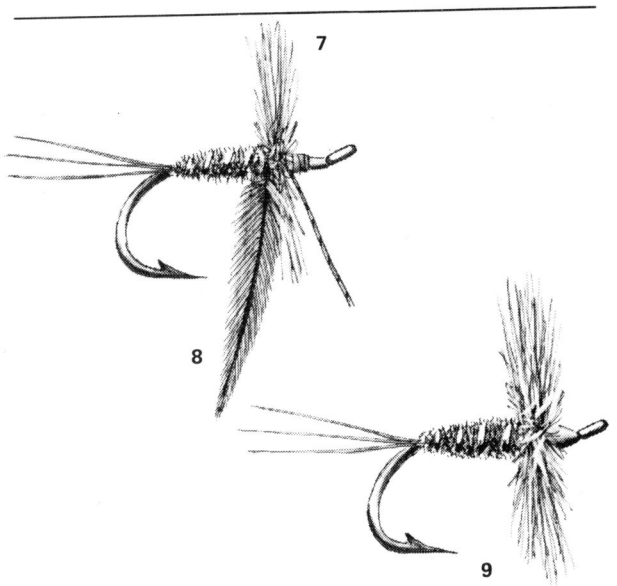

most insistent that the tying instructions be accurately conveyed, and so drawings of Nice's flies show the hackles tied in at the start of the operation, unlike most of the others.

Having placed a standard number 14 hook in the vice, take the silk for ten turns down the shank and tie in a natural bright blue-dun cock hackle, 1, followed by a further four turns of silk, when you tie in a dark red cock hackle, 2. Continue half way to the bend having trapped the stalks under the silk and at that point remove the ends. Carry on to the bend and as you do so tie in rusty-dun cock hackle fibres as the tail whisks, 3, and a length of fine gold wire, 4. Now tie in two pheasant tail herls, 5. Wind the silk back up the hook shank to the front of the red hackle, followed by the herl to form the body and rib with gold wire, 6. Wind the blue hackle, 7, to the body material, secure and tie off. Now wind the red hackle, 8, through the blue hackle to the front of the hook and secure, 9. Carefully whip finish the head and neatly coat with varnish.

This is a very durable method of tying a fly and one that can be recommended.

John Storey

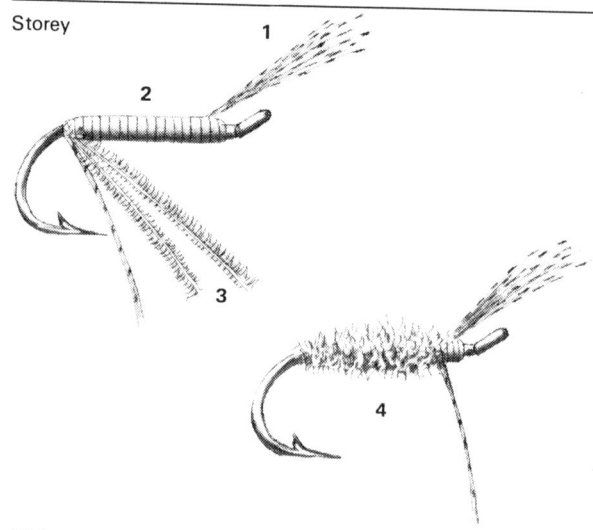

This north-country dry fly had its origins in a wet fly pattern of the same name. The original tying goes back to the mid eighteen-hundreds when a man called John Storey was the river keeper on the waters of the Ryedale Anglers' Club at Helmsley, North Yorkshire. The present keeper on that delightful river is Arthur Storey, grandson of John and it is interesting to note that members of that family have been keepers to the Ryedale club for the past 121 years. A remarkable record of service by one family to one club that even beats the Lunn dynasty on the Test in terms of years.

The original wet fly dressing had an underbody of fawn wool, the better to absorb water, and the mallard wing fibres sloped back over the peacock herl covered body. The fly has undergone a few changes down the years; for example at the turn of the century the dry fly had even reached this quiet little backwater on the Rye, and so the Storeys brought it into line by deleting the wool underbody, using a stiff cock hackle and setting the wings upright. It worked very well in its new guise.

A further change in the design came about in the mid-thirties when the fly started to sport a wing that had a very pronounced forward slope over the eye. Correspondence columns in the angling press have from time to time carried

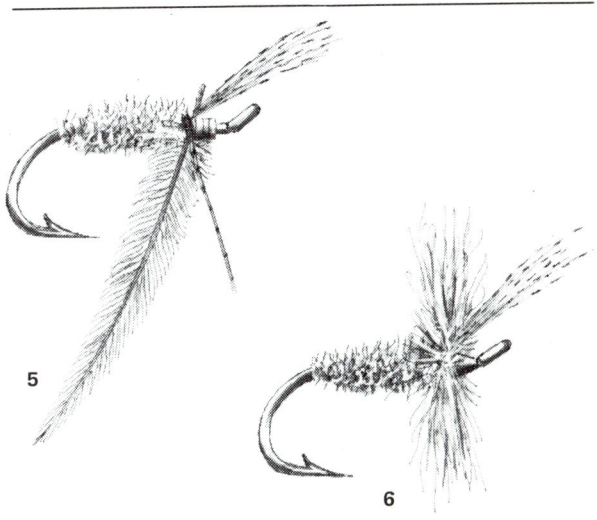

5

6

various theories as to why the wings are so slanted. Most of the opinions were far from the truth. The real reason is that when the present keeper started to tie the fly back in 1935, and at the time was "nobut a lad" he found some difficulty in tying upright wings! The members of the club did not mind for in fact so tied the pattern took just as many trout, if not more, and so it was decided to leave well alone. I obtained this information from Arthur Storey himself so I can vouch for the truth of it. He also confirmed that the pattern, in either its dry or wet form, was never intended to be a representation of a particular insect, it is simply a general pattern.

The hook size is usually number 14 or 16. Start the black tying silk down the hook shank and tie in a small feather from the breast of an adult mallard, 1. Continue the silk in even turns down the shank, 2, and at the bend tie in two or three strands of copper tinged peacock herl, 3. Wind the silk to just behind the wing, followed by the peacock herl to form the body, 4. Remove waste ends of herl. Tie in a sharp bright Rhode Island Red cock hackle, 5, and wind in place in the usual manner, 6.

I have seen patterns offered for sale with whisks and a gold rib. They are not true John Storey flies.

Jacques' Mayfly

Jacques

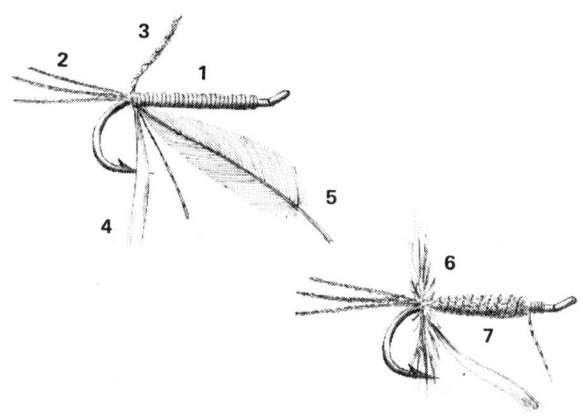

In 1965 A. & C. Black published a slim volume entitled *Fisherman's Fly* by David Jacques. In the main it was a compilation of his very good articles that had previously appeared in such journals as *The Field, Trout and Salmon* and the now defunct but sadly missed yearly publication *Anglers Annual* that for many years, under the editorship of Eric Horsfall Turner, and for its last four years of publication by Arthur Oglesby, had presented the cream of thoughtful angling writing to the public. That David Jacques should have featured almost yearly was to be welcomed for he provided a most analytical approach to fly fishing, and much valuable advice.

Like all angling authors, I doubt if Jacques made a fortune from his book. He did, however, have the satisfaction of writing within the 124 pages of *Fisherman's Fly* much sound comment that is worthy of study. I recommend the reading of his chapter entitled "The Mayfly" for he provides, or at least he provided to my satisfaction, the dressing of a mayfly which makes a lot of sense. A first glance at the illustration may cause one to think it a very strange contraption, but surely that is only because we have been conditioned by standard fly configuration. David Jacques put forward a most cogent argument for such a fly, based upon his observations of the natural dun when upon the water,

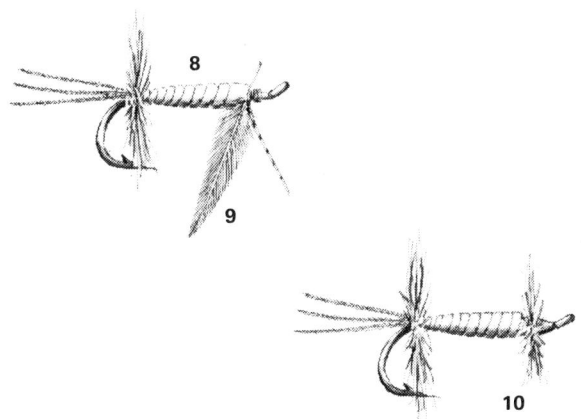

observations made over many years as a regular flyfisher on the River Test.

Space does not allow a full explanation of his theories and so I urge you to find a copy of his book and study at leasure. While my own experience of mayfly fishing is not so extensive as Jacques', I have nevertheless taken quite a few trout on flies so dressed, the trout's capture being all the more interesting because of the unusual fly design. I'm sure Jacques would not claim it to be the only mayfly artificial to carry in your fly box, but when the trout are being doubly difficult it is worth a try.

Take the red tying silk, 1, down the shank in close even turns and at the bend tie in three or four fibres from a cock pheasant tail, 2. Now tie in a length of reddish-brown floss silk, 3, followed by a length of natural raffia, 4, (I substitute raffine) and a large medium-olive cock hackle, 5. Wind the cock hackle around the shank near the bend on a short bed of silk and secure, 6. Now wind the reddish-brown silk to form the underbody, 7. Secure and remove waste. Wind the raffia over the underbody, 8. Tie in a light greenish yellow-olive cock hackle, 9. Do make sure it is much shorter in the fibre than the bend hackle. Wind in the usual manner, 10, and secure. Form a neat head and varnish.

Beacon Beige

Deane

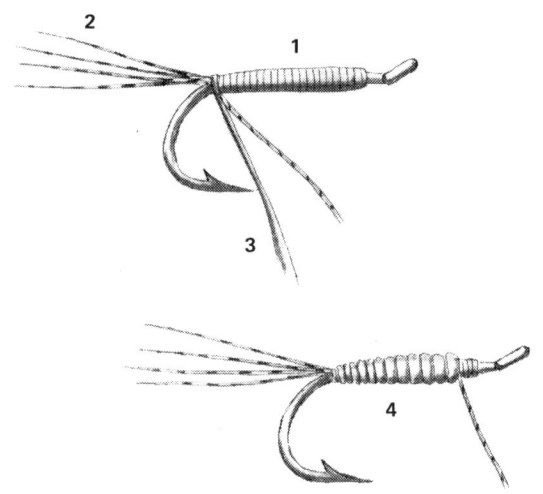

I am indebted to Peter Deane, a most knowledgable and skilled professional fly tyer who operates from Eastbourne, for the background to this highly popular dry fly. The pattern was originally known as the Beige, not Beacon Beige; the latter came many years after its inception. Its true origin lies in the year 1917 when a member of the Wills family of Dulverton was home on leave from the carnage of the Great World War then being contested over the shattered ground of the Somme. One can only hope that the fly's inventor had peaceful sport with it before being cast back into battle.

Long recognised as a capital trout taker in the Dulverton area, it gained wider fame when the late Frederick Tout, a well known tackle dealer in Dulverton, gave the dressing to Peter Deane just after the 1939 – 45 war when Deane was launching his fly-tying business.

Deane experimented with the fly for many a long hour on the river Culm in Devonshire, and after this period found that the fly's attractive qualities were bettered by the inclusion of a well-sprung Indian dark-red game cock hackle,

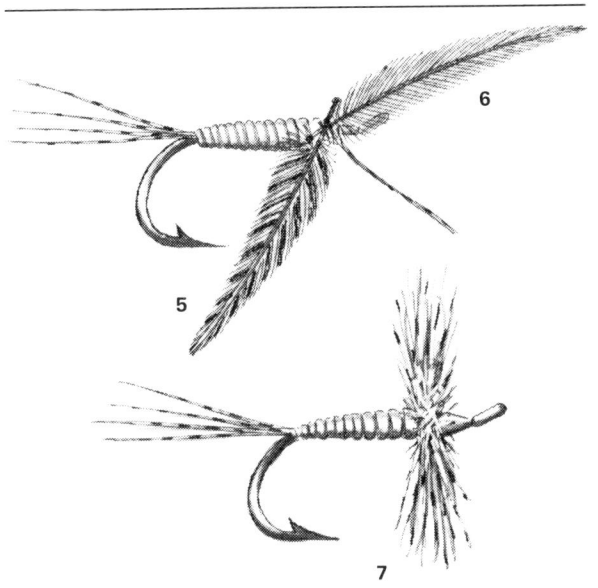

somewhat long in the fibre. So dressed the pattern works very well as a representation of the olive. Where did the name Beacon Beige come from? We shall now set the record straight so that future historians do not tear their hair to shreds seeking the reason. In the early years of Deane's venture into professional fly tying his workroom window looked out over the Culm valley towards Culmstock Beacon. There you have it. Simple when you know.

The pattern is straightforward. The hook size is 14 or 16. Take the tying silk, 1, down to the bend of the hook and there tie in four or more strong fibres from a Plymouth Rock cock hackle, 2, followed by a well-marked stripped peacock eye quill, 3. Wind the silk up the shank and then wind the quill to form the body, 4. Secure and remove the waste quill. Tie in a Plymouth Rock cock hackle, 5, and a dark-red Indian game cock hackle, 6. Carefully wind on to the hook shank, 7. Remove waste and finish off with a neat whip finish, and varnish.

Little Marryat

Marryat

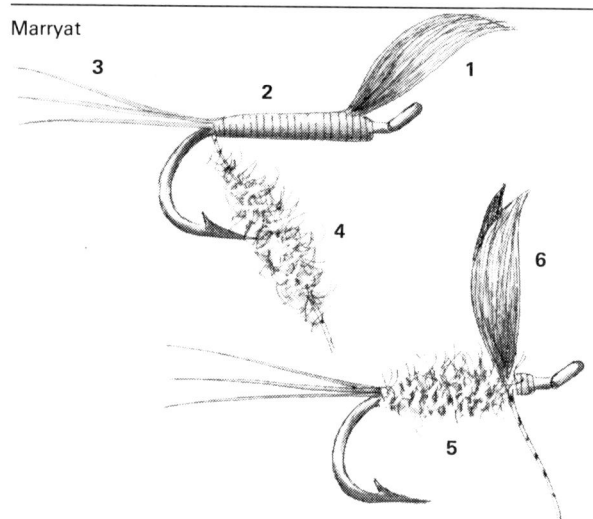

No book on dry flies would be complete without a fly designed by George Selwyn Marryat. He was born in 1840, the son of Colonel Marryat of Mapperton Manor, Hampshire, and spent the early part of his adult life in the Sixth Dragoon Guards, seeing service in India before returning to Hampshire in 1870 where, at the age of 30, he settled down to a life devoted to angling and the development of the dry fly.

Marryat was one of the first men to appreciate the advantages of the eyed hook and he collaborated closely with Henry Sinclair Hall on the development of such a hook. In 1879 a suitable design was achieved and we have much to thank the two men for. Marryat's specification for a hook was that it should have . . . "the temper of an angel and the penetration of a prophet; fine enough to be invisible and strong enough to kill a bull in a ten acre field."

The evidence that Marryat was the inventor of the split-wing style of dressing is, I think, conclusive. In a letter dated November 25th, 1882, he wrote of taking wing slips from opposite feathers to make upright split-wings. Prior to that date wings were bunched and the split effect was obtained by taking the tying silk through the fibres. It is also thought that he was the first man seriously to attempt the

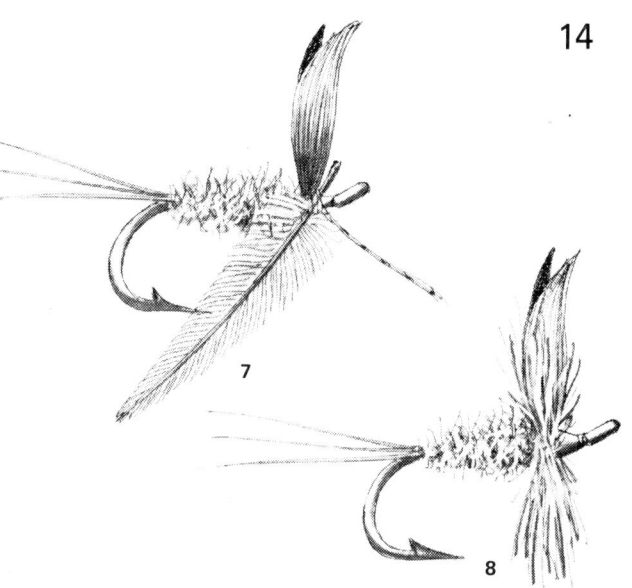

imitation of the nymphal form of the mayfly, and that he was the first to tie a female mayfly spinner with outstretched wings.

Possibly his greatest contribution to fly tying was when he worked with Halford to produce *Floating Flies and How To Dress Them*, in 1886. So great was Halford's debt to Marryat that he wished the book to be published under their joint names. Marryat declined, but it is true to say that without him there would not have been a book.

The Little Marryat is worth a chuck on waters far removed from the southern chalkstreams and I strongly advise you to try it. Start the tying silk down the shank and tie in two wing slips of palest starling, 1. Marryat frequently bleached such wings. Continue down the shank to the bend, 2, and tie in tail whisks of pale buff cock hackle fibres, 3. Wax the silk and dub it with Australian opossum fur, 4. You may well have to substitute here—a finely textured fur of a pale buff colour. Wind the dubbed silk to form the body, 5, and secure. Bring the wings into an upright position and divide with figure-of-eight turns of silk, 6. Tie in a pale buff cock hackle, 7, and wind behind and in front of the wings, 8. Complete with a neatly varnished whip finish.

Lunn's Particular

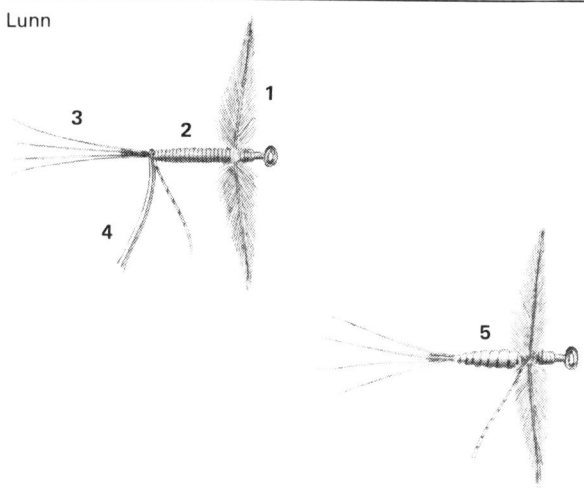

Devised by William Lunn, the famous river keeper of the Test at Stockbridge, this fly has been a top favourite spinner dressing of countless anglers for many years.

Lunn was born on January 2nd, 1862, in London, far removed from the trout stream where he was to make his reputation. At the age of 12 he ran away from home to work on a farm in Surrey. Despite a lack of formal education, his high level of intelligence caused him to question all aspects of country life and his natural aptitude for study resulted in him being appointed assistant keeper at High Ashurst at the early age of 15. By the time he was 20 he was the head keeper. In 1886 Herbert Norman, the secretary of the Houghton Club on the Test, asked Lunn to join them as a river keeper. At the time James Faithful was head keeper but he was nearing retirement and within 12 months Lunn was the head keeper.

He came to the Test at a time when great changes were afoot in angling techniques, though the Test fly fishers, destined to become leaders of the dry fly revolution, were somewhat slow off the mark. It is recorded that the first trout taken by a member of the Houghton Club on a dry fly did not occur until the year 1888. Such tardiness was more than made up for in the later years.

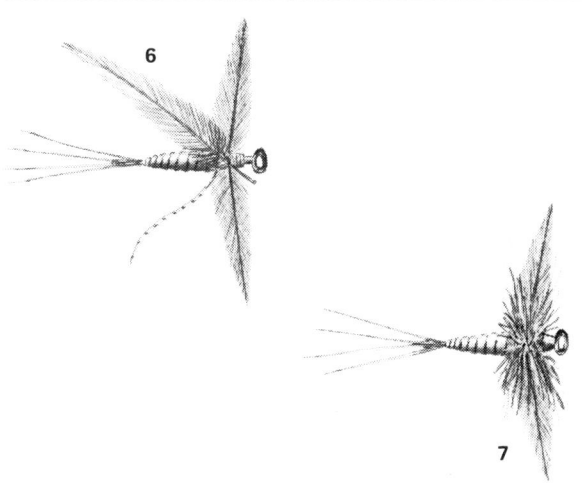

15

Lunn did not start to tie flies until 1916. He was introduced to the craft by E. A. Power, a man who was very impressed by Lunn's entomological knowledge and who considered that it should be translated into fur and feather. All Lunn's flies reveal one common factor: the use of very readily available materials. The Lunn's Particular was first tied in 1917 as a representation of the medium olive spinner and immediately earned a reputation on the Test as a capital trout taker. Since that time the fly has proved to be equally successful on all waters.

The fly is not difficult to tie but do take care over the size relationship between body and wings. The hook is generally size 14 or 15. Start the crimson tying silk down the hook shank and tie in two medium blue-dun cock hackle points, 1, tied flat. Continue the silk in close even turns to the bend, 2, and tie in four fibres from a Rhode Island Red cock hackle, 3, followed by a stripped stalk from a similar hackle, 4. Wind the silk back up the shank, followed by the stalk, to form the segmented body, 5. Secure and remove the waste. Tie in a medium Rhode Island Red cock hackle, 6, and wind behind and in front of the wings, 7, being careful not to distort them. Complete the fly with a varnished whip-finished head.

Yellow May Dun

Price

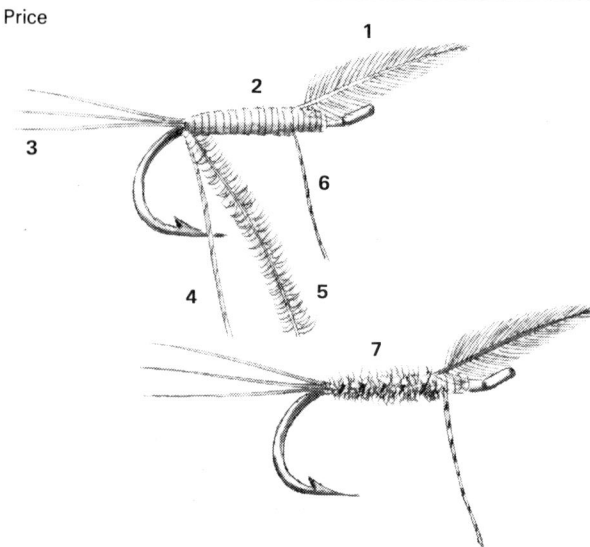

Any successful fly pattern devised by Taff Price must command our attention and respect, for Price is a very good amateur entomologist, expert angler and an innovative fly dresser. While his deserved reputation has been made mainly on still waters, we should not loose sight of the fact that he is also well versed in the ways of stream insects.

Price's championing of this fly, the *Heptagenia sulphurea*, that in the old days was known as the Little Yellow May Dun or the Yellow Hawk, may appear rather odd because it is not a fly well known to the majority of anglers. However, it does have its place in the fly-box, for when trout do latch on to the natural no other artificial is likely to tempt them. Taff Price recalls a day he spent on the Torridge when the trout would look at no other fly.

The naturals are quite common in most parts of the country, though I have rarely seen them at Driffield. Hatches are more frequent in the evening than during the day, with the duns more in evidence during May and June than any other month. Folk-lore has it that the trout rarely take the brightly coloured naturals but, as Price remarked, like all things in angling writing broad statements can often be disproved in the particular. Certainly I shall keep two or

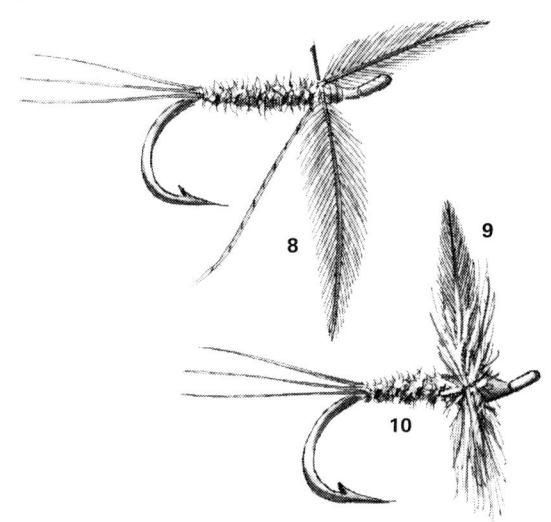

three tucked away in my fly-box for future use.

An interesting aside to Price's correspondence to me: he much prefers to rib with silk than wire, not wishing to add weight to a fly that is supposed to float. Obvious, but how many of us have considered that point?

To tie the Yellow May Dun use a size 12 or 14 hook. The thread specified by Price is Danville pre-waxed yellow. Start the silk down the hook shank and tie in two yellow hackle points for the wings, 1. Continue the silk down the hook shank, 2, and at the bend and tie in yellow cock hackle fibres for tails, 3, also a length of golden-olive yellow terylene thread, 4, and dyed yellow goose herl, 5, wind the tying silk back to point 6, follow by the goose herl, and rib, to form the body, 7. Tie in a dyed yellow cock hackle, 8. Now bring the wings into an upright position, 9, securing with turns of silk, then wind the hackle in the usual manner, 10, finishing off with a whip finish well varnished.

It is interesting to note that the fly shown in the colour plate is an interesting variation of this pattern, dressed on one of the new Swedish dry fly hooks. Tied by Price, the fly looks most effective.

Quill Gordon

Gordon

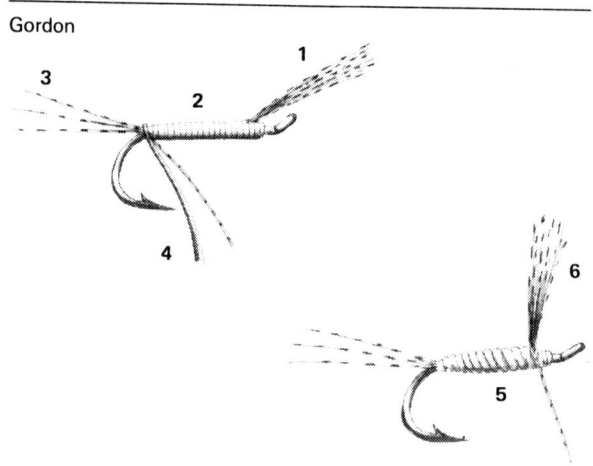

We now come to what must be the premier dry fly of America. It is worth spending a few words on the man who first tied it because I think it is fair to say that the craft of dry fly angling in that country can be traced back to him.

Born in Pittsburg, Pennsylvania, in 1854, Theodore Gordon's early life is not too well documented but he would seem to have been concerned with financial investment, a venture that crashed in 1893. Until 1900 he worked in a finance house in New York but then seemed to go into semi-retirement, moving to live with relations at Haverstraw, New York State, from where he made increasingly frequent fishing trips to the famed Catskill waters. In 1905 he cut himself loose, going to live in a secluded house within easy reach of such waters as the Beaverkill, Neversink, and the Willowmoc. Here he lived for the rest of his life, questing into the natural flies and their limitations.

A major influence in his life was F. M. Halford. In the winter of 1889 he obtained a copy of the master's *Dry Fly Fishing in Theory and Practice*. He started writing to Halford and in February 1890 he received a small package containing 48 dry flies. Theodore Gordon did not slavishly copy the flies but used them as the springboard to develop his own patterns based upon the natural flies of the American waters. Do not be put off because the Quill

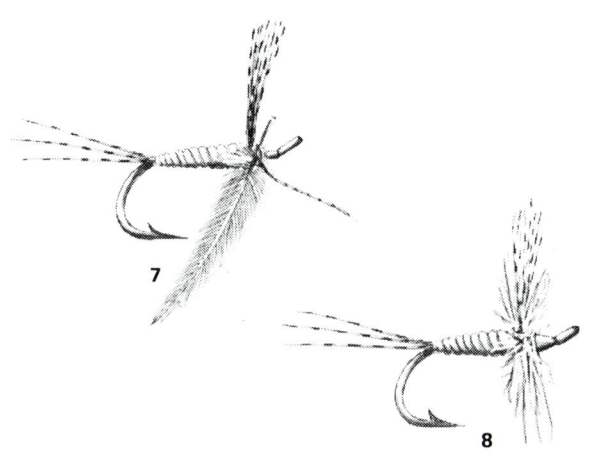

17

Gordon does not represent an artificial found on our own streams. I have found it a most excellent general pattern to use at any time.

Gordon died at the age of 61 in Bradley, close by the Neversink river he knew so well. He was buried in New York's Marble Cemetery in May 1915. His name was perpetuated in 1962 when the Theodore Gordon Flyfishers' Club was founded. Their slogan is ''Limit your kill, don't kill your limit''. Old Theodore would have approved of that.

The original fly was dressed on a number 10 or 12 hook, but for our waters I find a number 14 ideal. Start the cream tying silk down the shank. After a few turns tie in fibres from the feather of a summer duck, 1. Suitable alternatives are mallard fibres tinged brownish-olive, but very slightly. Continue the silk down the shank, 2, and at the bend tie in more summer duck fibres for the tail, 3, Now tie in a length of stripped dark peacock quill, 4. Later in the season a light quill is used. Wind the silk forward, followed by careful windings of the quill to form the body, 5. Secure and remove the waste. Take turns of silk round the root of the wings and bring to an upright position, 6. Tie in a dark blue-dun cock hackle, 7, and wind behind and in front of the wings, 8. Complete with a whip finish.

Goddard Caddis

Goddard & Henry

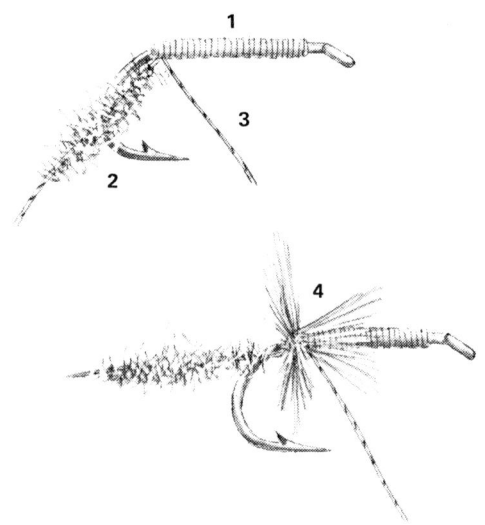

Some years ago when I was up to my ears in research for the fifth edition of the Courtney Williams' classic, *A Dictionary of Trout Flies*, I was in correspondence with that talented amateur entomologist and very good fly fisher, John Goddard. He provided me with much information and one particular fly took my fancy in no uncertain manner. It was the G. & H. Sedge, now known as the Goddard Caddis, the brainchild of Goddard and his companion Cliff Henry. It was designed in the first instance as a representation of *Glyphnotaelius pellucidus*, the mottled sedge, or any of the lighter sedges for its overall size and coloration can be varied.

Mainly a sedge of the stillwaters, the natural is usually active from May through to October, though Goddard indicates that the peak periods of activity are during late May and June, and again in August.

I was particularly attracted to this pattern because of its obvious floating ability, and by the novel method of tying-up the fly. It is not a fly the tyro should attempt, but for the more advanced tyer it should prove a most satisfying exercise in material manipulation.

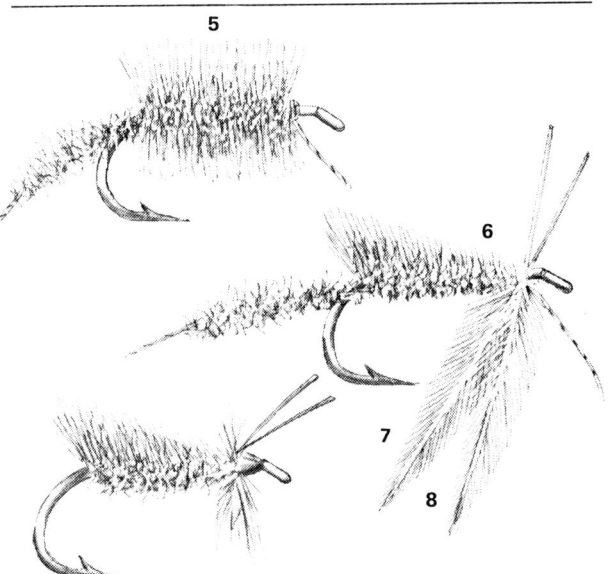

18

The hook should be either number 8 or 10, long shank. Having secured the hook in the vice wind the green tying silk, 1, down the shank in close even turns and there tie in a length of well waxed silk. Dub this silk with dark green seal's fur, 2. Make sure the dubbed silk is kept well away from the next operation. Take the tying silk, 3, and wind it round a bunch of deer hair. Pull tight and flair round the hook shank, 4. This is the same method as used in the well known Muddler Minnow. Continue to tie in and flair bunches of deer hair until it is fully covered, 5. Now take a pair of sharp scissors and carefully trim the deer hair into the silhouette of the natural fly, 6. Take care when you do for the damned hair goes everywhere. Wives hate it!

Carefully tie in two rusty-dun cock hackles, 7 and 8, ensuring that the trimmed stalks are pointing forward because you will use these to represent the antennae. Before winding the hackles stretch the dubbed silk under the body of the fly and secure at the head. Now wind the two hackles in the usual manner and complete the fly with a whip-finished head. Take the scissors and trim the top of the hackles into a sedge fly head shape, 9.

Golden Eyed Gauze Wing

Price

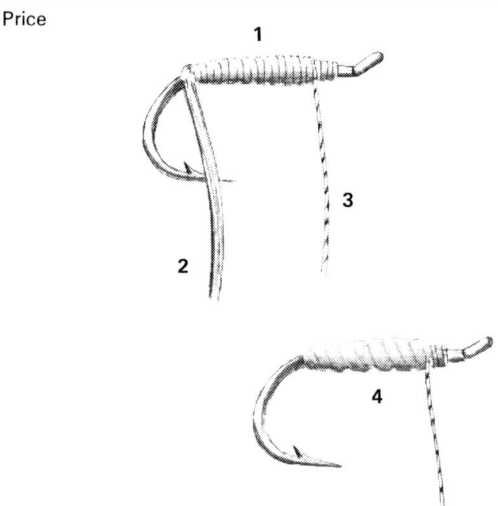

It may sound like the name of some dainty lady of pleasure in the Wanchai district of Hong Kong, but I do assure you that it is not! In fact it is a favourite fly pattern of Taff Price, the well known angler who brings an inventive turn of mind to his many patterns.

Price is quite right to admit that the Golden Eyed Gauze Wing is not a pattern you will use on every fishing trip. In fact he calls it a typical "tuck in the corner of your fly box" type of fly, to be used on those not frequent occasions when the very beautiful naturals are on the wing in sufficient numbers to attract the trout. Price is quite adamant that when the trout do start to take the natural you will not have a hope of matching the hatch without this fly; anything else looks drab in the extreme.

The most likely time for the emergence of this Hong Kong floosie is as dusk falls, which is the time I usually see a mirage of a large scotch and soda on the far bank, and which may explain why I continually miss the hatch. However, in view of the lateness of its emergence, Price has introduced a fluorescent element into the pattern to make it conspicuous in the failing light.

The inventor's method of winging is also worthy of note for he has found that artist's fixative sprayed on to raffine

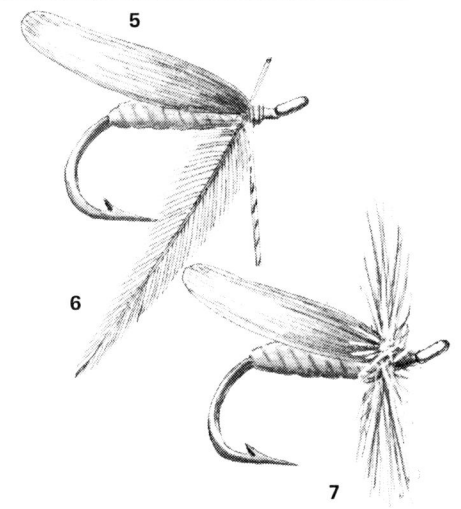

makes for a most durable wing. A word of explanation, artist's fixative is a liquid in an aerosol used for spraying over pencil or charcoal drawings. It gives a fine coat to the art work and prevents smudging. In fact the original drawings in this book were so treated. The great advantage of raffine sprayed with such a mixture is that it does not become flabby when damped. I suspect that Taff Price has hit upon an idea that will find great favour in winging many other dry flies. I shall most certainly do a great deal of experimentation with it.

Now to the tying of the Golden Eyed Gauze Wing. The hook size can be 10 or 12, long shank. Wind the pre-waxed yellow or green nylon, 1, down the shank to the bend and there tie in a length of fluorescent lime silk, 2. Return the tying nylon in close even turns to point 3. Now wind the lime silk to form a gently tapering body, 4. Take two pieces of lime-green raffine and cut to shape of the natural wing. Spray with artist's fixative and allow to dry. Carefully place in the required position and tie in, 5. Now take the green dyed cock hackle, 6, and wind over the base of the wings in the usual fashion, 7. Complete the fly with a whip-finished and varnished head.

Royal Coachman

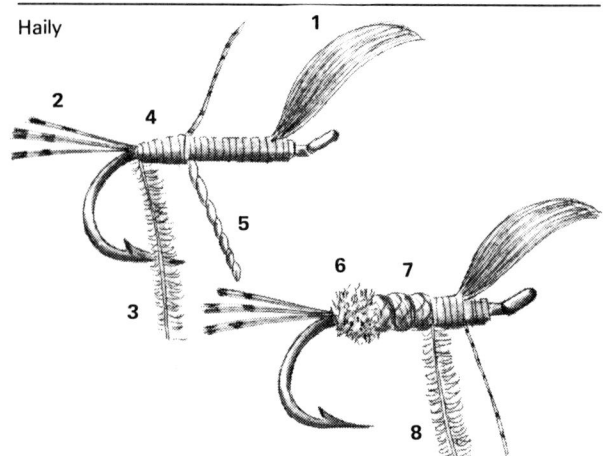

Haily

This pattern has a long ancestry for it can be traced back to the Coachman fly of the early eighteen-hundreds, a fly that was also known as the Harding fly. That erudite historian Courtney Williams was of the opinion that the first reference to the Coachman was to be found in Salter's *Angler's Guide*, fifth edition of 1823, and, with certain modifications, in Hofland's *Angler's Manual* of 1839, Kirkbride's book *Northern Angler* of 1840 and Fitzgibbon's *Handbook of Angling*, 1847. That the pattern was quoted with such regularity indicates that it was a true favourite.

Who was the original "Coachman"? It seems there are two views. One opines that he was Tom Bosworth, a coachman to George IV, William IV and Queen Victoria. The other view is that he was John Hughes, an angler living in Kent. I doubt if we shall ever be able to sort it out, but if any reader can help I shall be obliged.

Having being created in this country as a wet fly, it was not until it flew over the Atlantic that it became the Royal Coachman, and eventually a good dry fly for American waters. The change in the dressing seems to have been suggested by a Mr. L. C. Orvis and changed into fur and feather by a New York tyer named John Haily. The major change centred on the body of the fly. The standard Coachman had a body of bronze peacock herl, while the

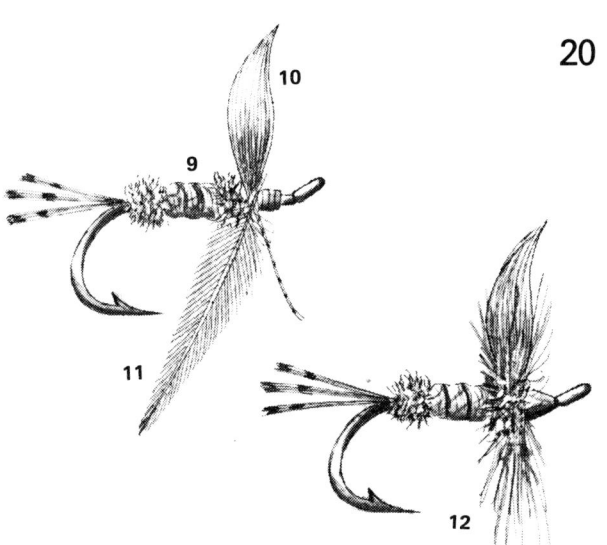

20

Royal Coachman had a three part body, plus tail whisks.

It was not until the early nineteen-hundreds that the pattern took on upright wings and a cock hackle. It then became a top favourite dry fly in the States, but it never seemed to catch on in the country of its birth when so dressed. I wonder why? Too gaudy? Perhaps. I do know that I have had great sport with it, and not only with daft stewbred trout, but the wild variety. One person of my acquaintence fishes the Test with virtually no other fly, and catches more trout than we mere mortals ever dream about. Do try it for I think you will be very surprised.

The hook is usually 12 or 14. It is easier to tie on a 12. Start the red tying silk down the hook shank and tie in two slips of white swan or goose wing fibres, 1. Continue the silk to the bend and tie in golden pheasant tippets, 2, followed by a length of bronze tipped peacock herl, 3. Wind the silk forward for one-third of the body length, 4. Tie in a length of scarlet floss silk, 5. Wind the peacock herl over the silk, 6. Take the silk forward a further third and wind the red floss silk, 7, securing and removing waste. Now tie in a further length of peacock herl, 8. Take the silk to the wing root, followed by the herl, 9. Bring the wing slips into an upright position, 10, and tie in a bright red cock hackle, 11. Wind the hackle, 12, and complete with a whip finish.

Pale Watery

R. Walker

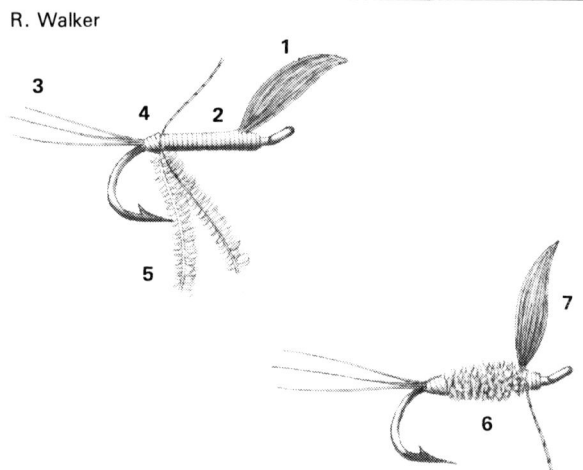

Few men have produced more words in the angling press and in books than Richard Walker. Like his opinions or hate 'em, you cannot ignore them, for he is a man of vast experience and practical knowledge, possessing an innovative turn of mind when he concentrates on fly design. I admit to always reading whatever Walker has to say. I do not always agree with him but in this instance I find myself nodding to his opinions. I refer to the vexed question of the best dressing for the range of pale watery duns, *Baetis bioculatus*. The natural fly is quite widespread throughout this country and on the waters I fish they put in a regular appearance, especially the chalkstreams where I have seen vast clouds of these flies, and the choice of a matching artificial was very often a hit and miss affair.

For years I pottered along using this and that pattern, but I quite freely admit that my ratio of presentation to catches was not good, until I lit upon Walker's tying of the pale watery. Can it be a question of faith in a particular pattern? Experience has taught me that confidence in a pattern plays a large part in its fish-taking ability. For example, the Gold Ribbed Hare's Ear is no doubt a cracking fly in other people's hands, but I have little faith in it, and consequently catch few trout on it. I look upon it as a "last hope" fly.

But we shall now turn to Richard Walker's pattern of

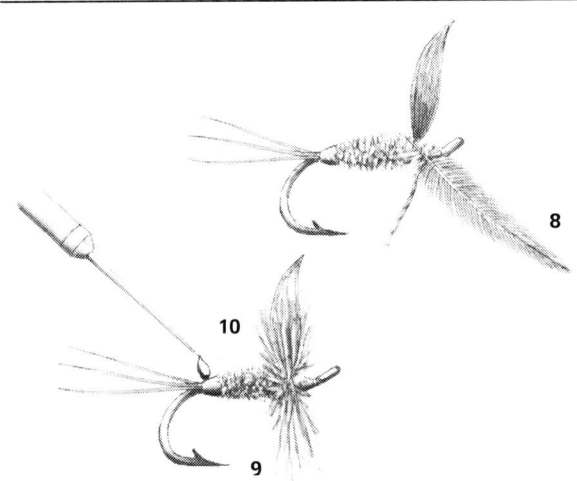

21

Baetis bioculatus. The hook size should be 16. Having placed the hook in the vice start the primrose tying silk down the hook shank and there tie in two slips of bleached starling wing feather fibres, 1.

Walker considers that the fly works equally well with a bunch of starling fibres tied in together and then split with the tying silk, or a bunch of cream or honey-dun hackle fibres tied upright. The choice is yours. I think on balance I prefer the hackle fibre wing.

Continue the silk in close turns down to the bend of the hook, 2, and there tie in whisks of honey-dun cock hackle fibres, 3. Now wind the silk forward for three or four turns, 4, and then tie in strands of swan secondary herl dyed a very pale greenish grey, 5. The colour could be so pale as to be almost white. Now wind the silk to the base of the wings, followed by the swan herl to form the body, 6. With the tying silk bring the wings into an upwards stance, 7. Tie in a honey dun or deeply tinted cream hackle, 8, and secure in the usual manner, 9. Complete the fly with a varnished whip-finished head. Take a drop of varnish on the point of a dubbing needle, spread the tail whisks and put the varnish at the roots, 10. This not only secures the tails in a splayed position but turns the silk at that point to a close approximation of the natural's end body colour.

Grey Wulff

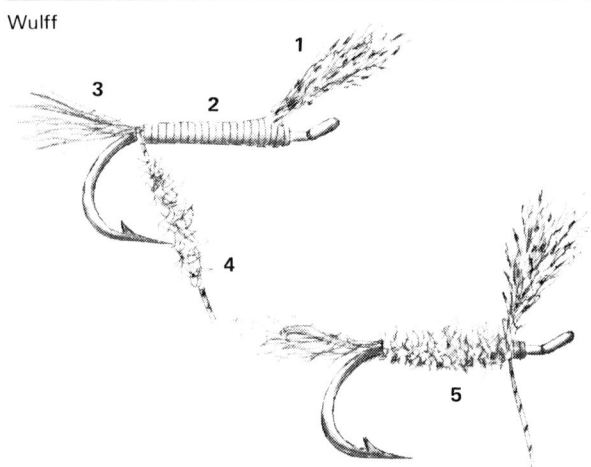

Wulff

A pattern that first saw the light of day in America. Devised by Lee Wulff, an angler of considerable repute, it came over to these shores in the early nineteen-fifties and was popularised by that excellent professional fly tyer, Peter Deane of Eastbourne. Peter Deane told me some years ago how it came about and the story bears repeating.

In the nineteen-fifties a client of Deane's, the late Lord Brand, was fishing the Houghton Club waters of the Test at Stockbridge with a guest, the then American Ambassador to this country, Lewis Douglas. It was the mayfly season and, as often happens at that time, the trout were being very selective, the patterns from Lord Brand's fly-box being totally ignored. A bankside conference took place, with the result that both anglers tied on a Grey Wulff apiece from the box of the ambassador. The effect was quite startling and both men were quickly into trout.

After leaving the river Lord Brand sat down and wrote to Deane, requesting rapid fly production and enclosing an example of the pattern that had worked so well. The next day Peter Deane examined the fly, noting the forward slant of the undivided wing, lying forward in a single tuft. He rapidly reproduced the pattern and sent examples post haste to the Test. The mayfly were still damnably selective but his tying did the trick.

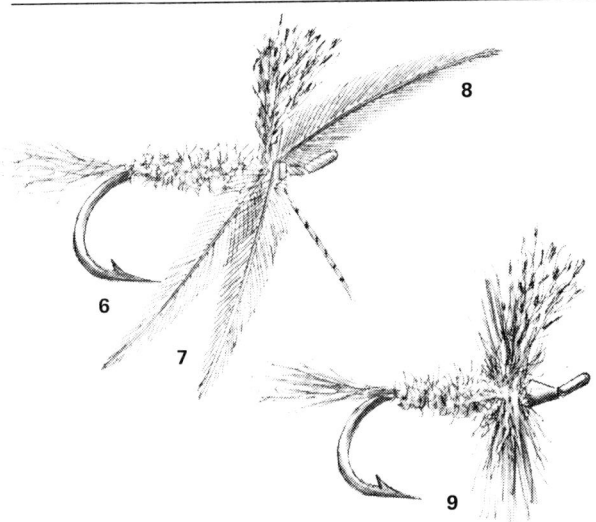

22

The word got around over the years and now Deane confirms that his tying of the Grey Wulff is a consistent best seller to those who fish the mayfly waters. My own experience is that it is in the top league of such patterns.

While it is a dry fly the trout no doubt accept it, with its for'ard facing wing, as a stage in the evolution from nymph to dun when the wings are not fully emerged from the cases, the veins not yet fully blooded, and consequently a fly that is easy prey. Surely an inducement to any trout?

The Grey Wulff mayfly is tied on a hook size 10 to 8, standard shank, not long shank. Start the yellow tying silk down the hook and tie in a bunch of brown barred squirrel tail fibres, or grey squirrel tail fibres, 1. Continue the silk in close even turns down the shank, 2, and at the bend tie in whisks of natural brown bucktail, 3. Now dub the silk with grey squirrel fur, 4. Wind the dubbed silk to form the body, 5. Tie in two blue-dun cock hackles, 6 and 7, and one dark-red Indian game cock hackle, 8. Wind so that they are well mixed, 9. Complete with a whip finish.

A smaller version tied on hooks between 16 and 12 is dressed with whisks of small brown barred squirrel tail fibres and only one hackle of dyed medium blue dun.

Iron Blue Dun

Origin unknown

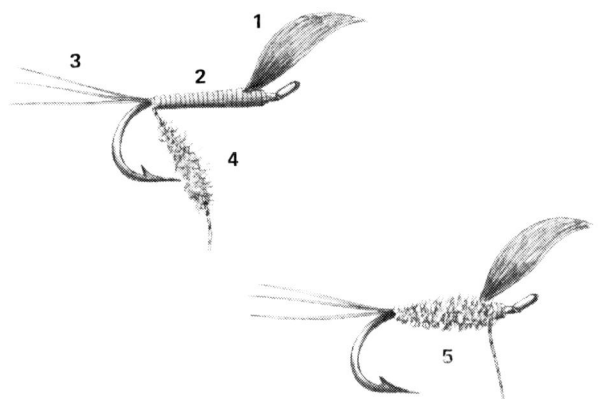

To attempt a description of a typical Iron Blue Dun artificial is almost impossible, for almost every fly tyer down the ages who ever put pen to paper had his own variation of this fly. Not to be outdone by all those who have gone before I will now add my own two-pennyworth and confuse the issue still further. The Iron Blue Dun which I now describe was one of the very first patterns I ever tied. Where I obtained the dressing I can no longer remember, though I suspect that it must be of East Yorkshire origin. I do know that I have never had cause to try any other dressing and if we examine one of the natural species, *Baetis pumilus* or *niger*, compared to the pattern I dress, I think you will see a similarity in hue.

The natural fly has a body that ranges from a very dark brown-olive to a greyish black. The wings are of a greyish-blue colour, while the tails are a dark grey. Legs show a distinct olive-brown colour. The fly is widespread throughout the British Isles, being common on both alkaline and acidic streams. They are to be seen early in the season from April to June and again at the end of the season.

For some reason only an entomologist may be able to explain, they revel in the cold wet and windy weather which usually greets the start of every season. I recall an opening

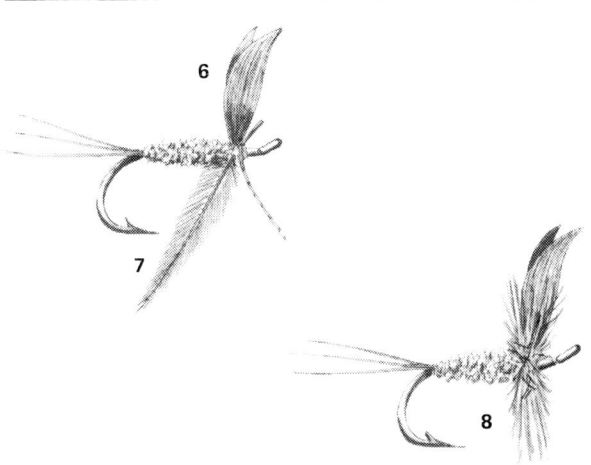

day on the River Colne at Fairford when it snowed heavens high and yet the naturals, and my artificial, were welcomed by the trout like manna from heaven. Only such interest kept me on the snow-blown banks and away from the bar at the Bull and a large whisky.

Many years have now slipped by since I first tied this fly but I have never had reason to doubt its efficacy, or the inclination to tie any other version. The hook size is 16. Start the dark red tying silk down the hook shank and tie in wing slips of starling wing feather fibre dyed a greyish-purple colour, 1. Continue the silk in close even turns down the shank to the bend of the hook, 2, and there tie in tail whisks of natural blue-dun cock hackle fibres, 3. Well wax the tying silk and dub very sparingly with a dark greyish-olive seal's fur mixed with a minute pinch of purple mohair, 4. Wind the dubbed silk and form a neatly tapered body, 5. Secure and remove the waste dubbing material. Bring the wing slips into a more upright position, 6, and secure with figure-of-eight turns of tying silk, ensuring that the slips are well separated. Now tie in a real top quality hackle dyed a dark olive-brown colour, 7, and wind both behind and in front of the wings, 8. Finish off the fly with a neatly whip-finished head and a smooth coat of varnish.

Daddy Longlegs

R. Walker

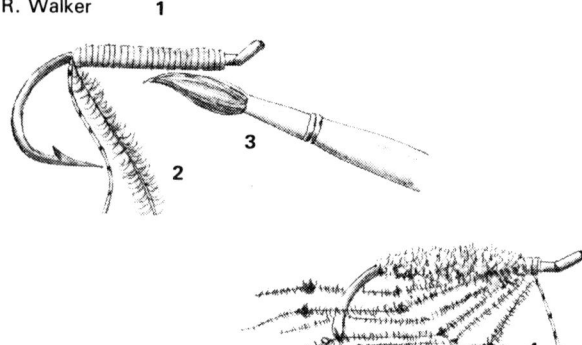

I really must be a late developer in terms of flyfishing because the worth of the Daddy Longlegs, or crane fly, came to me late in life, the summer of 1976 to be exact, when conditions must have been ideal for the procreation of this strange insect. The meadows of the chalkstream where I usually fish were alive with the beasts. When the wind blew them on to the water in droves the trout gave every indication of preferring this leggy insect to the exclusion of whatever else was passing by. I realise that the behaviour pattern was not the norm, but it did indicate that a few Daddy Longlegs in my fly-box would not go amiss. Subsequent years have proved they have a certain place in my armoury.

Generations of anglers have tied various representations of the crane fly. W. H. Lawrie in his book *A Reference Book of English Trout Flies*, 1967, put forward the view that the tenth fly described by Dame Juliana Berners in her book *Fysshinge With An Angle*, 1496, was in fact a crane fly, though he also opines that it could have been a wasp! Leonard West in his rather finely illustrated book of 1921, *The Natural Trout Fly and its Imitation*, mentions three patterns of crane fly; the Large Crane Fly, the Orange Crane Fly and the Evening Crane Fly. Personally I would not consider it necessary to tie up such variations, for the number of times such insects are on the water, or more particularly attracting the trout, is not great. I have now learn-

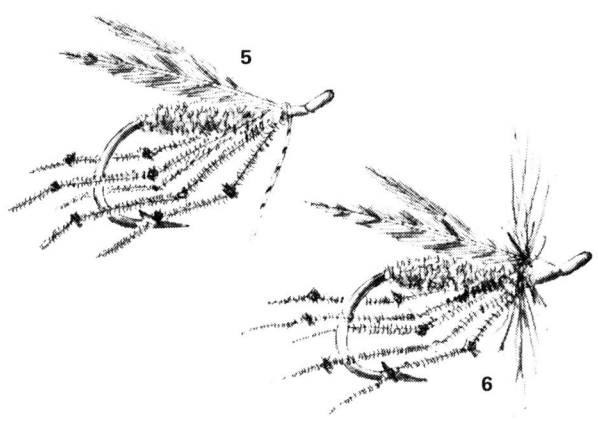

ed my lesson and whenever a Daddy Longlegs skitters about on the surface then I am ready for it.

My favourite tie is not from the dim and distant past but one developed by Richard Walker just a few years ago. No doubt there are other equally effective patterns but I enjoy tying this one and that is all part of the fun of fly fishing. Walker recommends that the pattern be cast out and allowed to lie inert when stillwater fishing, or if used on the river allowed to float down without drag. Personally I give the creature a wee tweak now and again so that it acts in the manner of a sedge, believing that it brings it to the attention of the trout.

The tying is a bit complicated, but great fun. The hook is between 6 and 10, long shank. Take the light brown tying silk, 1, down to the bend and there tie in a length of swan secondary feather fibre dyed a muddy cork colour, 2. Wind the silk forward and coat the turns of silk with varnish, 3. Now twist the swan fibres together and wind over the wet silk to form the body. Allow to dry. Take a selection of pheasant tail centre feather fibres, the longest ones, and knot each one in two places to simulate the "knee joints". Tie in so that they slope backwards, 4. Tie in two cree cock hackle points for wings, 5, sloping backwards. Tie in a ginger cree, or plain ginger, cock hackle quite long in the fibre and wind over the wing roots, 6. Complete the fly with a varnished whip finish at the head.

Polymay

R. Walker

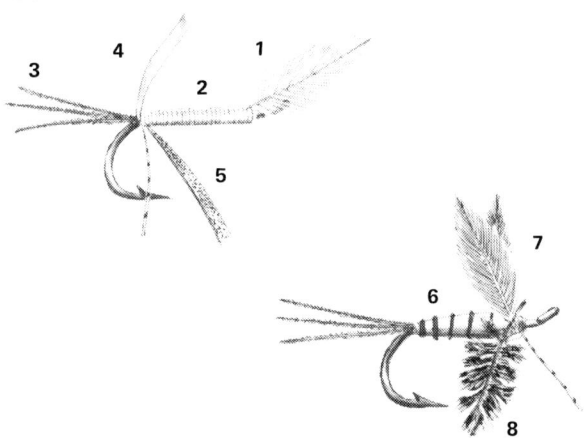

Like the previous pattern, the Polymay is one of Richard Walker's creations. I hope those readers who do not have ready access to mayfly waters will forgive the inclusion of yet another pattern in this book, but I do know quite a few people who have found it a great fly. Incidentally, it is not only the chalkstreams that have the mayfly, though quite a few folk think that to be the case. I could take you to a simple little stream that flows down from the Yorkshire moors where in late May and early June you would be hard put to take a trout without a mayfly pattern on your leader.

However, having already described David Jacques' unique tying of the mayfly, also Peter Deane's Grey Wulff, I promise this will be the last. One of the Polymay's major features is its excellent floating capability, always a problem with a large dressing, brought about by the use of polyethylene foam. When properly tied and given a good soak in floatant, the pattern is almost unsinkable.

Now to the tying. The hook specified by Richard Walker is a fine wire long shank number 10. Having placed the hook in the vice start the medium-brown tying silk down the hook shank in close even turns, tying in two cock hackle points for wings that have been dyed a pale sea-green colour, 1. Continue to wind the silk down the hook shank, 2, down to the bend and there tie in the tail whisks 3, which

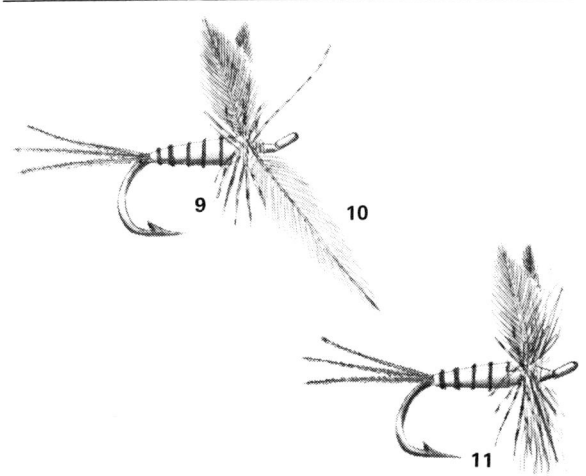

are from the centre tail feather of a cock pheasant. Now tie
in a length of straw-coloured raffine, 4, remembering that
this material must be pre-damped before use, followed by a
strip of polyethlyene foam, 5.

Wind the polyethlyene foam up the hook shank to form a
neatly tapered underbody. Walker in fact ties the strip in at
the base of the wings so that he can have one winding down
the hook shank and one back again to the wings. The
choice is yours and depends on how thick you want to final
body shape to be.

Now carefully wind the pre-damped raffine over the
polyethlyene to form a neat covering. Maintain the tension
on the foam and the raffine and start to rib over with the
tying silk. The ribbing should show two distinct wide bands
of brown silk at the tail before winding in the usual open
spiral all the way up the body. Secure the foam and the raffine and remove waste ends, 6. Now bring the wings into an
upright position, opening out into a shallow "V" and
securing in place with the tying silk, 7. Tie in a brown partridge hackle, 8, and wind in the usual way, 9. Remove
waste stalk. Now tie in a long fibred top quality ginger cock
hackle, 10, and wind behind and in front of the wings, 11.
Secure and remove waste hackle stalk. Complete the fly
with a whip-finished head, neatly varnished.

Last Hope

Goddard

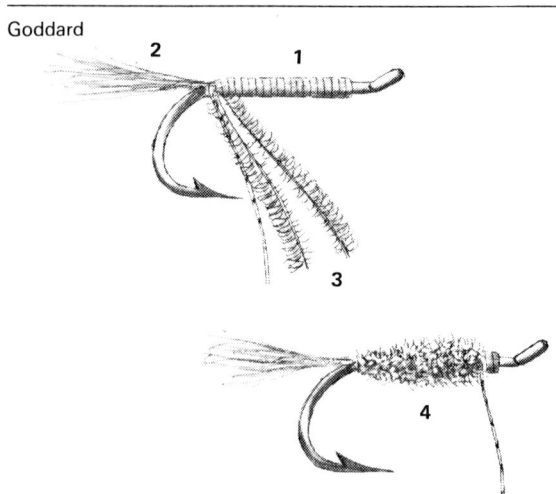

I have already described a pattern by John Goddard, namely the Goddard Caddis, and it is time we looked at another
from his stable, an artificial I value above most others. We
all know the frustration and almost total rage that comes
over us when the beastly caenis descend, setting on our
clothing, rods, even lines, while the trout ignore all our
small offerings as we try to imitate the little cream insect.
Well, I do not claim that John Goddard's Last Hope will
always be the answer at such a time, but it is an artificial
that goes a long way to keeping down my own blood
pressure.

The Last Hope was originally tied by Goddard as a
representation of the pale watery dun, *Baetis bioculatus,*
but as I have said it proves most effective as a caenis. The
artificial should always be tied on very small hooks and it is
very essential that only the smallest and shortest fibred top
quality hackles should be used. Such hackles are not always
easy to come by and so in this instance it is quite permissible
to trim the fibres of a longer hackle with a sharp pair of
scissors.

Ideally the body should be dressed with two or three herls
of a dark stone colour, or alternatively of a light buff
shade. Goddard specifies the source as the Norwegian
Goose, but if not available heron or condor herl can be

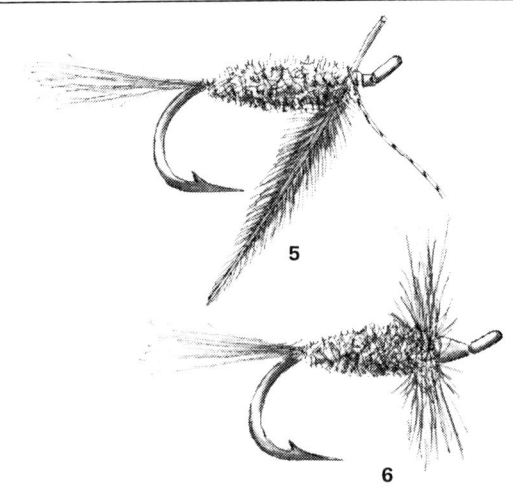

26

5

6

substituted. As the condor is now a threatened species, I suggest you use heron.

At this point may I make a plea to all fly tyers, especially the newcomers to the craft, to use commonly available materials and not to create a demand for feathers for birds that are under environmental pressures. After all, Lunn tied highly efficient patterns from materials found in any farmyard, and the trout, I'm sure, cannot differentiate between, for example, the wing made from hen blackbird fibres or dyed starling fibres. Having said that, do not ignore the small corpses one finds on the roads!

Remember when tying the Last Hope smallness and neatness are the watchwords. The hook is 17 or 18 and of fine wire. Start the pale yellow silk, 1, down the hook shank in close even turns to the bend and there tie in at least six fibres from a honey dun cock hackle, 2. Having secured the whisks tie in the herls, 3. Wind the silk back up the hook shank, followed by the herls, twisted together, to form the body, 4. Secure with the tying silk and remove the waste ends. Tie in a very short fibred stiff cream or honey-dun cock hackle, 5, and wind in close even turns towards the eye, 6. Tie off and remove waste hackle. Complete the Last Hope with a carefully wound whip finish, and varnish.

Kahl Sedge

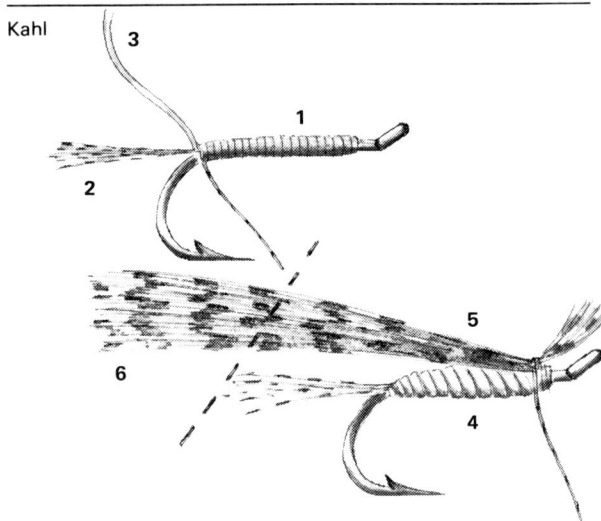

Kahl

It has been my distinct pleasure to have played host to Milton Kahl, one of the most skilled, and likable, American fly fishers it has been my pleasure to know. To see Milt in action is to be reminded of a heron. He is tall and somewhat stooped and will spend a day not moving from his chosen position on the stream, occasionally flicking out his, to our eyes, awfully long leader, all 18 feet of it, which falls in an induced "mess", but gives the fly many feet of travel between the weed beds before drag sets in. Much further than my ten foot leader would allow.

I well recall a day with Milt on the Derbyshire Wye. Sport had been spasmodic and the weather had been awful. We stood in front of a roaring fire in the Peacock at Rowsley, thawing out with a couple of large whiskies. Suddenly Milt said, "Don, I have decided that fly fishing is the most enjoyable thing a man can do standing up"!

On another occasion we were fishing with him and two other friends on the Bull water at Fairford in the Cotswolds. The day was over and Milt suggested that as it was our last night together we should "dress up" for dinner. But of course, we all said, wishing to retain the last vestige of the Raj tradition, and praying that my wife had packed me a dark suit. We assembled in the bar, the gels in

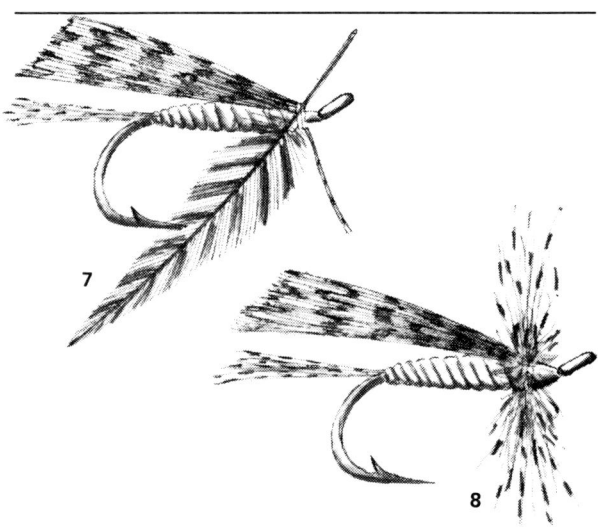

long dresses, Douglas and I in suitably sombre suits and white shirts. Milt strode in wearing the most bizarre jacket I have ever seen, made up from dozens of small squares of different tweed checks, all of a brilliant colour. His trousers were bright green with a red holly-berry motif all over them. Thank God fly fishing is not a totally serious business! Come back soon, Milt.

The fly I now describe is Kahl's own dressing and has found great favour with many American fly fishers. I can also vouch for its effectiveness on waters far removed from the Hot Creek of the High Sierras where it was developed.

The hook is between 14 and 20, but for our waters stick to 14. Take the white tying silk, 1, in close even turns to the bend. There tie in a bunch of grizzly cock hackle fibres, 2, as the tail, followed by a length of stripped peacock quill, 3. Take the silk forward, followed by close even turns of the peacock quill and form the body, 4. Remove the waste end and secure. Now tie in a rolled wing of mallard flank feather 5. Having tied in the wing clip off the rear end at an angle and level with the tail, 6. Now tie in a top quality grizzle hackle, 7, and wind over the wing roots, 8. Finish off the fly with a neat varnished head.

Grayling Fiddler

Horsfall Turner

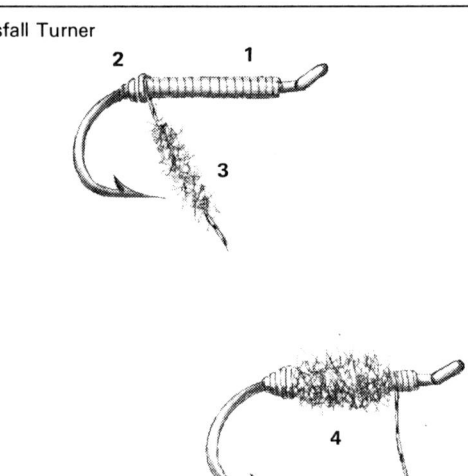

I am indebted to that doyen of fly fishers, Eric Horsfall Turner, for his tying of a most excellent fly for when one is chasing the grayling of the northern streams. I have been a friend of Eric for more years than I care to remember. Together we have wandered the banks of the Yorkshire Derwent, the Pickering Beck and the Costa chalkstream, casting a fly here and there, and I can honestly say that after each visit I was wiser about the ways of the trout and grayling than before. Horsfall Turner's analytical and contemplative views on fly fishing and fly tying are well documented in his book *Angler's Cavalcade*, 1966, and should be required reading by all who would know the finer points of our craft.

The Grayling Fiddler came to my notice in 1968 after a day chasing grayling in East Yorkshire. I had had a damnable day. The fish were just not taking firmly, seemingly intent on infuriating this angler by their habit of gently nipping the fly but not taking with any degree of firmness. Time after time I struck only to see the usual bubbling swirl as the fish turned down. That evening I shared a pint with Eric and told him of my infuriating day which brought me only three brace. He chuckled, and produced from a small

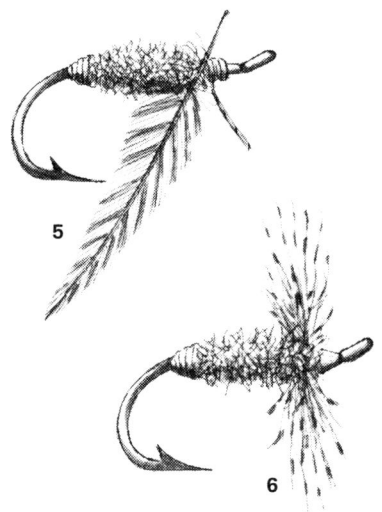

28

5

6

box a couple of tiny flies. "Try these" he said, "and let me
know how you get on".

The next morning saw me again on the late autumn
banks. Grayling were bubbling under the far bank. My
usual Red Tag brought me a few fish but then they started
this business of just touching the fly without taking firmly.
I changed to the Grayling Fiddler, without much hope of
success I must confess, yet the fish took it with firmness.
Not every time I admit, but with a far greater frequency
than any other pattern in my box. Why? well I really do not
know, though perhaps that is how it should be, for if we
knew all the answers surely the fun would go out of fishing.

The dressing is quite simple. Take the brown tying silk in
close even turns down the number 18 hook shank, 1, and
having reached the bend make three or four turns back up
the hook shank, 2. Re-wax the tying silk and sparsely dub
with teased out red wool, 3. If fished late in the day chop-
ped up red fluorescent wool can be added to advantage.
Wind the dubbed silk to form a neatly tapered body, 4.
Secure and remove the waste dubbing. Tie in a very small
sharp grizzle cock hackle, 5, and carefully wind to create a
bushy hackle, 6. Remove waste hackle stalk and complete
with a neatly varnished whip finish.

Grey Duster

Origin unknown

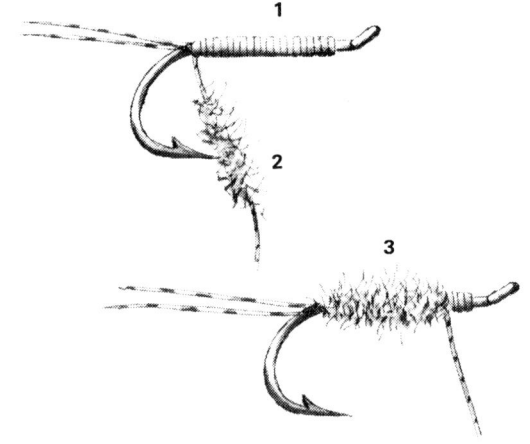

This must surely be one of the best known dry flies in the anglers fly-box. The late Courtney Williams was a great champion of this pattern and in his book, *A Dictionary of Trout Flies*, indicates that he was introduced to the fly on the River Alwen in Wales, being told by the locals that it was the only pattern he would need when fishing that river. He went on to say that the Grey Duster accounted for nine out of every ten fish he took while staying in the area. Either he was brainwashed into total confidence in the fly—and that can happen—or else it was truly just what the trout wanted. Unfortunately he did not tell us what the natural fly on the water happened to be that day.

Personally, I have always thought of this fly as a very good general pattern, though if leaning in any direction it is towards the pale watery tribe. I would tell you of a day on the Coln at Bibury some years ago when the trout were picking off olives that floated down to them. My usual artificials were ignored, even my sheet anchor, Kite's Imperial, was treated only to a casual glance by a fish I had set my heart upon.

What to do? Having nothing to lose I tied on a Grey Duster. The trout took it, I struck, and half way to the net the trout came off, going to ground in a weed bed. Damn

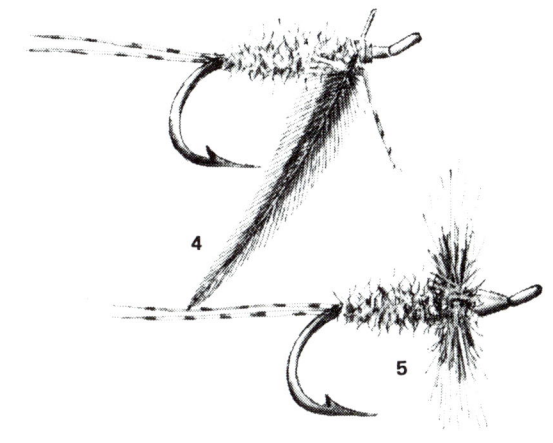

it. I sat and had a smoke thinking that was the end of it. Without any hope I cast the fly over the weed bed to where I could just make out his rear end. The fly sailed down past the bed, he turned and followed it and then he was on. No mistake this time, and in short order I had a nice brown trout going just short of two pound on the bank. So much for the old folk-tale of a pricked trout sulking for the rest of the day.

On rivers the length and breadth of the country I have found the Grey Duster to be an excellent fly, frequently doing the trick when so-called imitations of the natural fly on the water have been totally ignored. Yes, a truly favourite fly.

The hook is usually between 14 and 16. Take the brown tying silk, 1, down the hook shank in close even turns. At the bend tie in well marked badger hackle fibres for the whisks, followed by dubbing the tying silk with rabbit's fur of a bluish hue, 2. Carefully wind the dubbed silk to form a neatly tapered body, 3, not too dense. Tie in a good quality badger cock hackle, 4, and wind in close turns to complete the fly, 5. Remove the waste and whip finish at the head. The original dressing did not have tail whisks, but I like 'em. The choice is yours.

No-Hackle Fly

Swisher & Richards

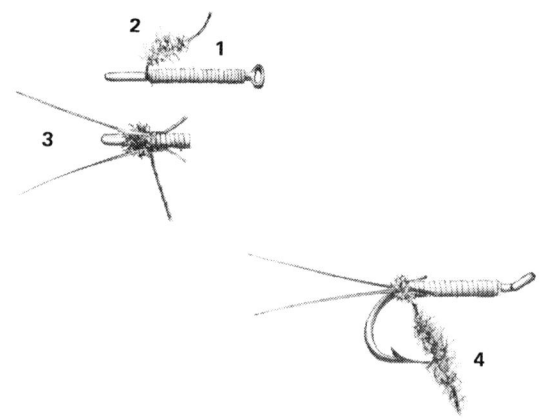

Over the centuries there have been few major design changes in the artificial trout fly, until some few years ago two talented amateur entomologists and anglers in America sat down and re-thought fly design. They were Carl Richards and Douglas Swisher. The results of their observations and trials were published in *Selective Trout*, 1971, a book that caused quite a stir across the Atlantic. Since that time their designs of flies without hackles have become firm favourites with many U.S. fly fishers and therefore such patterns are worth investigation in this book.

The theory behind the design is based upon the originators' belief that the traditional hackle, especially on smaller hooks, masks the parts of the fly that cause the trout to take, namely the body and the wings, and that if one could dispense with the hackle and still have a good floater, such a design would be an improvement. While I have not experimented to any great degree with these patterns, many thoughtful fly fishers have done so, with most encouraging results.

To tie a hackleless winged dry fly presents certain problems, not least how to stop it falling on its side on the water, and how to ensure that it will not sink. Swisher and Richards indicate they have overcome the latter problem by using for the body polypropylene fibres, a material that has a specific gravity of 0.94 and so floats very well indeed. The

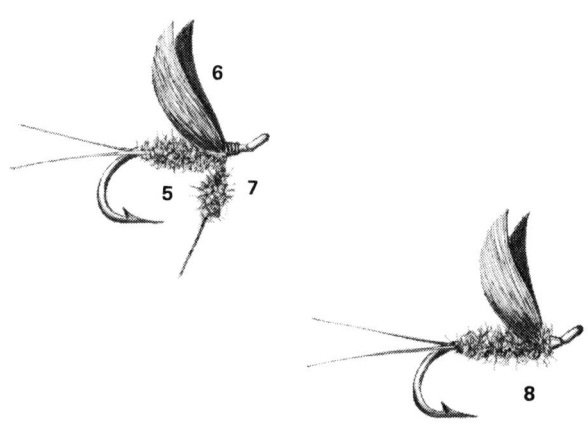

stability of the pattern was achieved by the tying method described below. I have not specified the particular colours of the materials as one can use this dressing style for any of the duns. The hook size therefore is also a matter of choice, though I would say that I have seen exquisite examples tied on number 22 hooks!

Having placed the hook in the vice wind the tying silk in close even turns, 1, to the bend. There dub the silk with a minute amount of poly dubbing, 2, and wind round the hook for two or three turns. Now place the tail whisks at either *side* of the shank, 3, and secure. The wedge of dubbing should splay them outwards, to act as outriggers when the fly is on the surface. Redub the silk, 4, and wind to form a body, 5. Take two wing slips and tie in at the *side* and towards the bottom of the shank, with a "V" spread to the wings. Usually the wings also slope slightly to the rear of the hook, 6. The angled wings, placed at the bottom of the shank, are an essential part in allowing the fly to fall gently, like a parachute, and when on the water aid upright stability. Redub the tying silk and wind in front of the wings, 8. Complete the fly with a neatly varnish head.

My own experiments have shown that correctly dressed flies float very well in an upright manner. I am sure there is much scope for further experimentation.

Blue Winged Olive

C. F. Walker

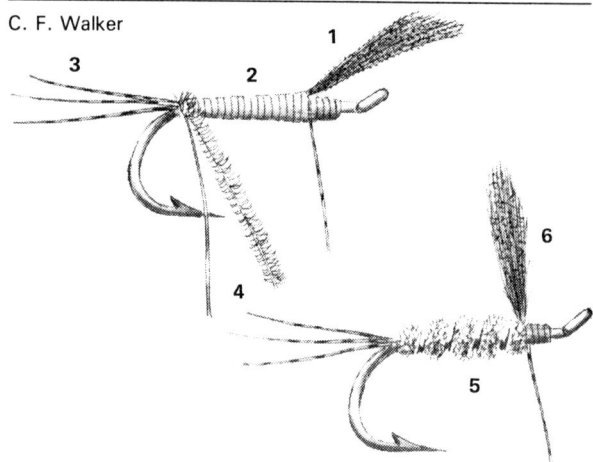

The natural blue winged olive, *Ephemerella ignita*, must surely be the first streamside insect the budding entomologist can recognise without too much difficulty. A largish fly with blue-grey wings, three pronounced tails and an olive coloured body, it is found all over the British Isles and is a common fly on the chalkstreams.

It is understandable that such a common fly has been imitated countless times in fur and feather, under many names, and has given rise to much discussion in angling literature as to the best dressing. It is not an easy fly to imitate. The perfect pattern that rose trout after trout yesterday is just as likely to be totally ignored today, and one is hard put to pin down the reason.

G. E. M. Skues, though generally thought of as the master nympher, was also a highly skilled dry fly angler and he devoted many years to the study of the B.W.O. and the search for the ideal dressing. One pattern that will always be associated with Skues is the Orange Quill, for though Skue did not invent it, it seems it may never have reached prominence if he had not rescued a single pattern from a Winchester tackle dealer in the late eighteen-nineties. To cut a long story short he found the dressing—pale starling wings, bright red whisks and hackle, with a body of stripped condor herl dyed hot-orange—ideal when the B.W.O. was about at dusk. The body colour is certainly a long way

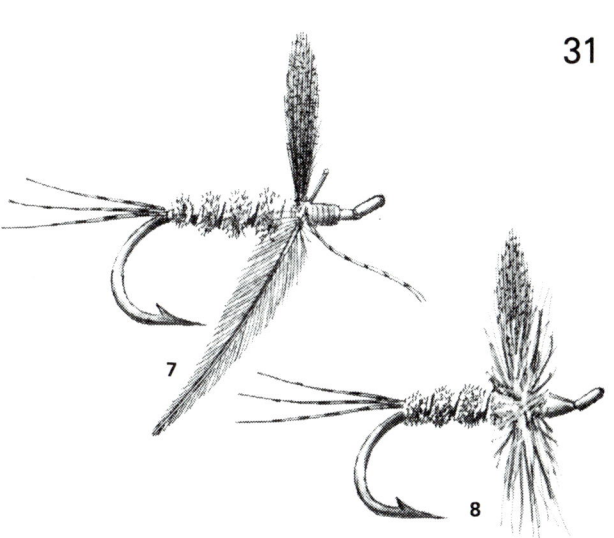

from the dun, but it is a good approximation of the female B.W.O. spinner, commonly called the sherry spinner.

It would seem obvious to assume that the trout take the Orange Quill for the spinner and not the dun, yet at dusk they take just as avidly when spinners are not evident. We have a lot to learn about trout optics. Despite the forgoing I, and many other anglers, find the Orange Quill quite useless during the daytime, and so over the years I have looked for a few decent B.W.O. dun patterns I can use before dusk. One of my favourites is a pattern devised by Commander C. F. Walker, an angling author with a string of books to his name and great experience on the chalkstreams.

I always tie this pattern on a number 14 hook. Start the yellow tying silk down the hook shank and tie in a bunch of fibres from the breast feather of a waterhen, 1. Continue the silk to the bend, 2, and there tie in fibres from a speckled partridge breast feather, 3, followed by a length of fine gold wire and a length of blue-grey condor herl that has been dyed olive in picric acid, 4. Wind the herl to form a neatly tapered body and rib with the gold wire, 5. Bring the wings into an upright stance with turns of silk, 6. Tie in a good quality cock hackle dyed yellow-olive, 7, and carefully wind behind and in front of the wings, 8. Finish off with a neatly whip-finished head, and varnish.

Pope's Nondescript

Pope

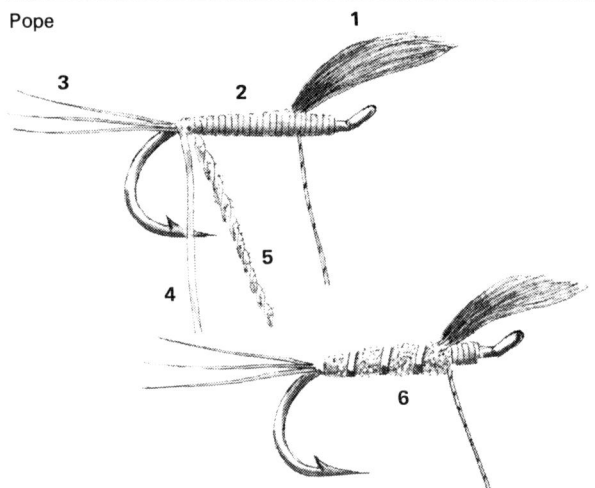

I wonder just how many fly patterns have been invented since the dawn of fly fishing. It must be an astronomical number and the vast majority have been swept away down stream after a few moments' glory, never to be heard of again. Others have grown to be recognised classics with names known even to non-anglers, while a third category hover in the background, famous in their day and cropping up periodically in angling literature. Pope's Nondescript comes into the latter class.

Some while ago research caused me to re-read a number of books in my library that have their origins in the turn of the century, and I became aware that this fly was regarded by many of the old school as a cracking pattern. In a spirit of curiosity I dressed a few, trying them some weeks later. The result was very gratifying and I wondered just why the pattern had almost followed the dodo. From that day I have used it regularly, and so have quite a number of friends. After receiving free samples and trying them, the Pope's Nondescript now has a place in their fly boxes. It would be nice to think of an old pattern being given a new lease of life.

G. E. M. Skues wrote in quite glowing terms about the fly, commenting that he found it to be very effective when the trout were tailing, or at the start of a hatch. He also sug-

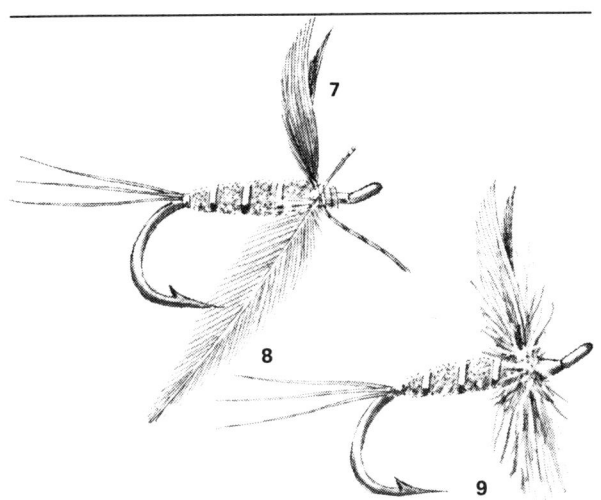

gested that it was a capital fly when fished sunk! Frankly, I have not found it particularly useful for tailing fish, but as a general pattern it serves me well.

It was devised in the late eighteen-hundreds by W. H. Pope of Dorchester, a man who numbered among his friends such giants as F. M. Halford, G. S. Marryat, H. S. Hall of eyed hook fame, Major Turle, whose name is perpetuated in the Turle knot, and Dr. Wickham, the inventor of the Wickham's Fancy. Pope died in 1908, no doubt safe in the knowledge that the dry fly cult would last for ever. What he would have made of some modern stillwater lures does not bear contemplation.

The dressing is quite easy. The hook size is 16 or 18. Start the pale green silk down the hook shank and tie in wing slips of light starling fibre, 1. Continue the silk down to the bend, 2, and tie in tail whisks of red cock hackle fibres, 3, followed by a length of flat gold tinsel, 4, and a length of light green floss silk, 5. Return the tying silk to a point just behind the wings. Now wind the floss to form the body and rib with the flat gold tinsel, 6. With the usual turns of silk bring the wings into an upright position, 7. Tie in a bright red natural cock hackle, 8, and wind behind and in front of the wings, 9. Secure with a whip finished head.

Wake Fly Sedge

Price

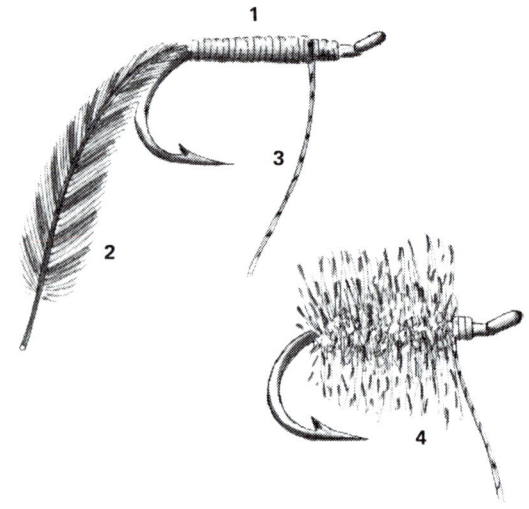

Another pattern from the vice of Taff Price and one of his own favourite dressings. I must confess that it is a most satisfying beast to tie and I have spent many happy hours busking up the many different colour variations which, after due trial, will I'm sure enter my own favourite-fly list.

Price told me that it is a broad spectrum pattern that imitates nothing in particular, yet appears to the trout as a winged insect on the surface making strenuous efforts to reach the safety of the bank. He believes the fly is frequently taken by trout to be a species of *lepidoptera*, the moth family, but whatever they do take it for, Price is more than happy with its overall performance.

Its true home is the many stillwater locations around the country. The method of fishing is to cast out a fair distance and then retrieve, "waking" it back with long steady pulls across the water surface. Taff Price has also had success with the pattern when river fishing at dusk. Casting across, he allows the fly to float with the current, and as drag sets in and the fly begins to skitter across the surface it imitates very well the struggling efforts of the sedge. He has also

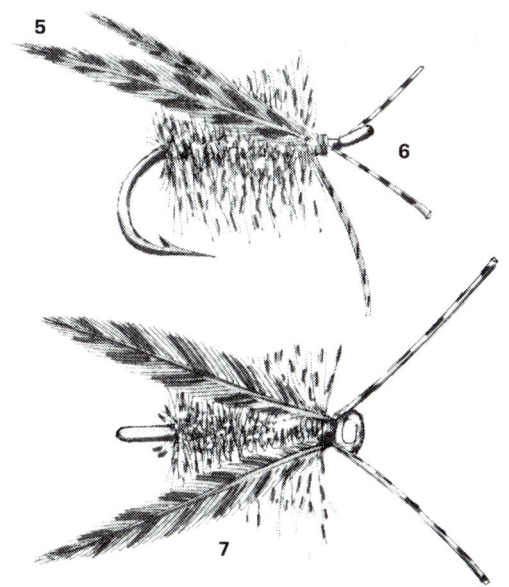

taken sea-trout by this method and so it is obviously a good all-rounder.

One can tie up various colour combinations of this pattern, black, brown, etc., but the one here described is the Grey Wake Fly Sedge.

The hook, generally long shank, is between 10 and 12. Having placed the hook in the vice start the black tying silk (Price specifies the pre-waxed variety) down the hook shank, 1, until the bend is reached. There tie in by the tip one or more grizzle cock hackles, 2, and then return the silk in close even turns back up the hook shank to point 3.

Taking the hackle in the pliers wind closely up the hook shank, 4, securing and removing the waste material. Tie in two grizzle cock hackle points, 5, well splayed delta fashion and pointing rearwards. Do not cut off the hackle stalks that protude forward but carefully arrange them to simulate the antennae, and secure, 6. Carefully whip finish the head between the hackle stalks and varnish same. The fly when viewed from above should appear as figure 7.

Misty Blue Dun

Waites

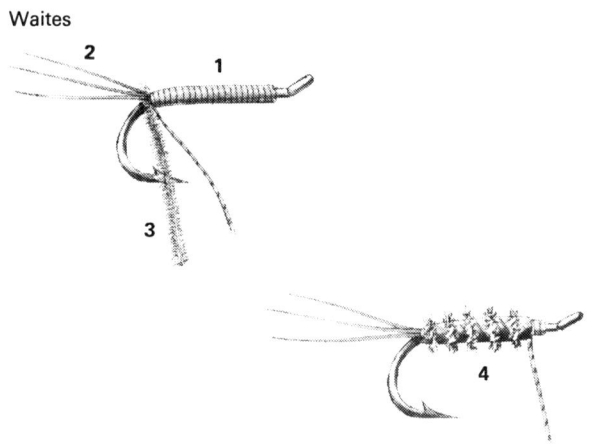

Any man who spends his working life on a good stream is a person we should, if we have any sense, listen to and learn from. Such a man is Tony Waites, head keeper on the Driffield chalkstream in the East Riding of Yorkshire.

Tony Waites is one of that small number of people who seem to be able to think like a trout. They said the same of old William Lunn on the Test. His powers of observation are quite unique, aided by 10/10 eyesight which allows him to identify with ease the dun or spinner sailing under the far bank. Such eyesight really comes into its own when nymph fishing. Admittedly the water is gin clear, but nevertheless to see the precise moment of take many feet upstream and two or three feet down, is beyond my goggle-assisted eyesight.

Let me quickly recount a day at Driffield some seven years ago. My wife and I were fishing the Island Beat on a hot morning in August. The trout were nymphing and proving very very difficult. While we munched a sandwich in the shade Waites arrived and I suggested he took my rod. He tied on his own Spurwing nymph and we watched with interest as he merged with the bankside grasses and gave a perfect demonstration of how to take and release five long-range brown trout without moving more than 15 yards. Such is the measure of the man.

Some years ago he took a particular interest in devising a

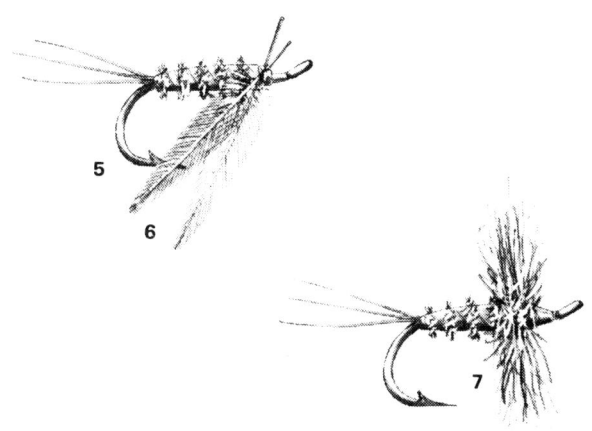

dressing of the medium olive. After a few months of experimentation, he came up with the Misty Blue Dun. To save future historians wracking their brains trying to discover why the name Misty is tacked on to Blue Dun, I will now give the answer. It is simply that Waites has a rather pale labrador dog called Misty, a most friendly old fellow who makes quite a ritual of christening the four wheels of my car whenever I arrive at the stream!

Now to the fly. The hook size is either 14 or 16. Take the yellow tying silk in close even turns down the hook shank, 1, until the bend is reached and there tie in three long fibres of a light blue-dun cock hackle, 2, followed by a single strand of natural blue-grey heron herl, 3. Wind the silk in close even turns to the starting point and then rib with the heron herl, 4, allowing the underbody of yellow silk to just show through between the ribbing. It is an advantage to coat the silk thinly with clear varnish before ribbing for this makes its more durable and turns the silk to a light olive shade. Having completed the body tie in a light brown cock hackle, 5, and a light blue-dun cock hackle, 6. Wind together, maximum number of turns, 7. Finish off with a neatly varnished whip-finished head.

While this fly will not withstand the ravages of many trout, it is one pattern where I gladly exchange durability for effectiveness.

Kai-Fly

Pitt

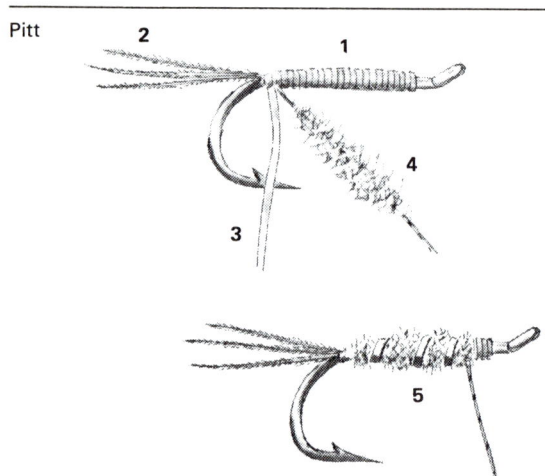

For quite a long while I have been in correspondence with Colin Pitt, a man who shares my passion for collecting angling books—especially the rare volumes and for the history of fly tying. Over this period we have written at length on many aspects of fly design and so I was pleased to receive from him a nicely tied example of his Kai-fly.

The name? Well, like so many other patterns down the years, the fly has a personal association in that the name Kai is that of his Afghan hound that provides the basic body material. When I received the first pattern I was impressed by its overall appearance and subsequent river tests have proved that it is indeed a capital general purpose fly in the tradition of the Imperial and the Dogsbody.

Devised late in 1975, it was still in good time that season to bring Pitt 23 excellent trout from a reservoir near his home in Rochdale. Since then he has taken many fish on the Kai-fly from Ladybower Reservoir, Draycote and Llyn Alaw in Anglesey. It has also given good service as a river fly on such northern waters as the Wharfe, the Lune and the Ribble. A fly that consistently takes fish from the Wharfe has to be good. For fast tumbling waters the fly has the advantage of being high-riding and easily visible, a plus factor when the take of a trout can so easily be missed in such conditions.

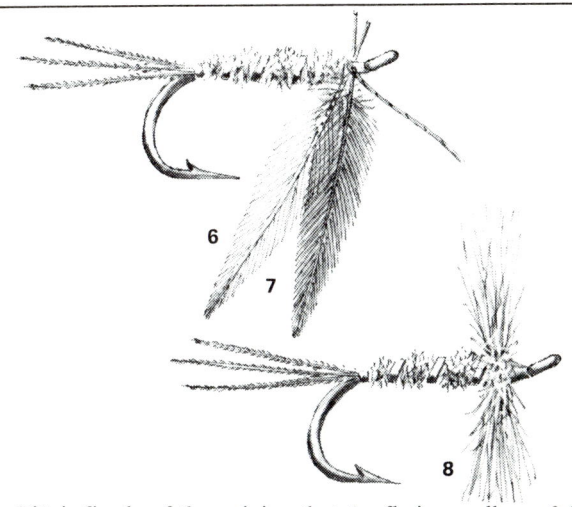

35

Pitt is firmly of the opinion that the fly is equally useful for grayling and gives instances of good bags from the River Wharfe. He also dresses a nymph version, substituting the cock hackles for a hen and tying a thorax of pheasant tail herl.

The dressing is easy, though you will have to cultivate the friendship of an Afghan hound owner! The hook is quite large, number 10 or 12. The tying silk should be light brown or grey and is wound down the shank in close even turns, 1, to the bend of the hook. There tie in three or four strands of cock pheasant centre tail feather fibres, 2, followed by a length of flat gold tinsel for the rib, 3.

Wax the silk and dub with the underhair of an Afghan hound, 4. This hair is, I am told, waterproof, a fact I had not realised previously. Alternatively you can take a few long hairs and wind them round the shank in place of the dubbed silk. In fact the fly in the colour plate was so tied by Pitt. Having wound the body material rib it with the flat gold tinsel, 5. Tie in two good cock hackles, 6 and 7, one a natural red or dark ginger and the other a cream colour. Wind together, 8. Complete the fly with a whip finish and varnish the head.

Ridsdale's Favourite

Ridsdale

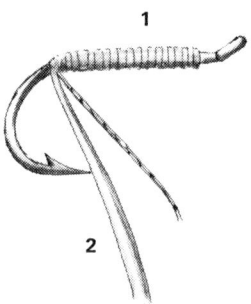

This pattern always has a place in my fly box. It is a simple fly for the beginner to tie, yet one that has done great execution for me on small rivers and becks. Strange to relate, I had tied and used it for years without knowing who had invented it until a correspondent sent me the details.

It was first made generally known to the public by the late Yorkshire angler, Tim Wilson, who wrote a regular column called "The Story Behind the Fancy" for the magazine *Angling* back in the nineteen-forties and early fifties. In the March 1950 issue he gave the history of this deceptively simple pattern and I'm sure by doing so helped a lot of anglers to many fish.

First devised in 1938 by Austin Ridsdale, a native of that beautiful area known as Wharfedale, the pattern quickly gained a local reputation as a good fish catcher. It was born of an idea when he was fishing the Mickley area of the River Ure. He noticed the trout were particularly partial to what he described as a "yellowish fly". Wilson put forward the opinion that it may have been one of the pale wateries. Over some weeks Ridsdale experimented with various combinations of material, all of a grey or yellowish tinge, until he finally settled on the simple dressing here described.

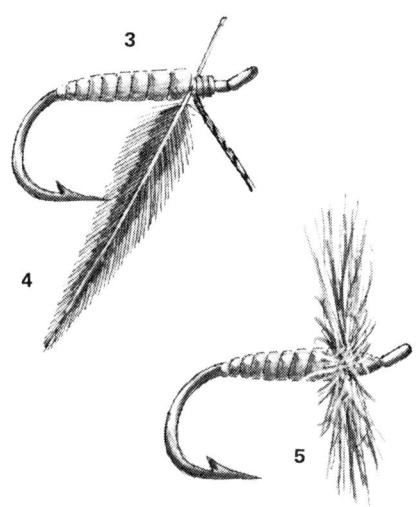

36

I have very strong recollections of a grand day on a Northumberland river when a "yellowish fly", which I could not identify, was engaging the attention of every trout in the area. Presenting my usual selection brought but scant success, but when I changed to Ridsdale's Favourite my luck also changed and creeled a decent basket of fish. Since that time I have had other occasions on which to bless the fly, but only on fast flowing, tumbling waters.

Though the original dressing specifies natural raffia the fly works equally well with the more up to date raffine, but do remember to pre-damp it. The tying is simplicity itself. Place a number 14 or 16 hook in the vice and in close even turns take the crimson tying silk, 1, down to the bend of the hook. There tie in a length of raffia, 2. Wind the silk back up the body and follow with close even turns of the raffia to form the body, 3. Now tie in a good quality light badger or creamy-grey cock hackle, 4, and wind around the hook shank, 5. Ridsdale stipulated that the red tying silk should show at the head for a few turns. For good measure I usually use red varnish on the whip-finished head, though I doubt if it matters one jot.

Little Claret Spinner

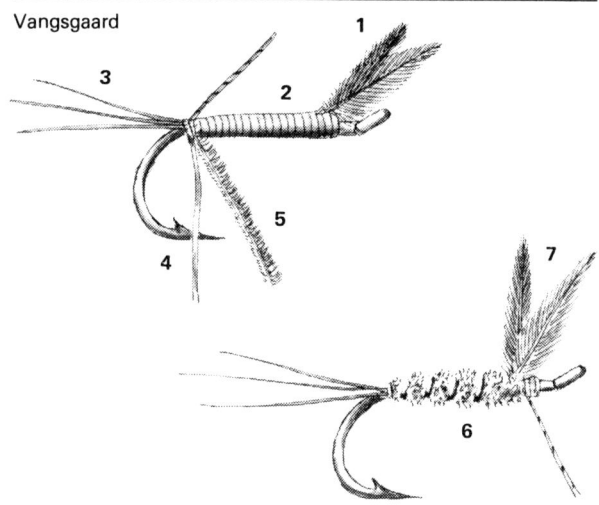

Vangsgaard

During my long friendship with the Dane, Preben Torp Jacobsen, I have many times had cause to thank him for fly-tying tips and wrinkles passed on to me, and for certain fly dressings that while unknown on this side of the North Sea are old established favourites in Scandinavia. I do not claim that all the patterns are effective on British waters, but there is one pattern I always have in my fly-box, the Little Claret Spinner, devised by one of the old school of Danish fly tyers, Johs Vangsgaard of Odense.

It is many years now since Preben sent me a sample of this dry fly and I have used it with regularity ever since. Though called Claret Spinner, the wings are not tied flat, but semi-spent. In this fashion they represent both the dun and the spinner—a good old compromise! The coloration of the artificial bears all the hallmarks of *Leptophlebia vespertina* and as such the pattern should really be more use on the stillwaters. I would not quarrel with that, but I have seen those insects in considerable numbers on streams and rivers in the early part of the season, and have had fine sport with this artificial when they were about.

I think it is also interesting to note that I have used this fly to good effect in the late evening when the B.W.O. spinner has been about on the stream. I appreciate that the dark

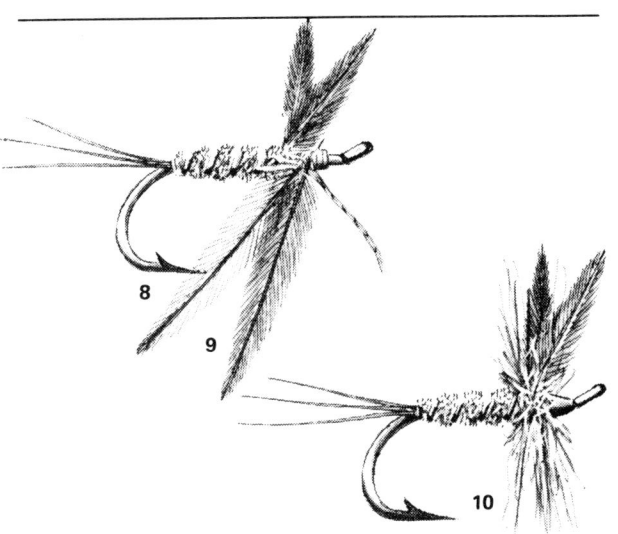

brownish-red condor herl does not look, to our eyes, like the lobster red colour of the blue winged olive spinner, nevertheless the fly at that time seems quite attractive to the trout. I have also found it a good general pattern when pottering about the weedy margins of stillwater in the late evening. For the grayling it has proved useless.

Now to the tying. The hook size is 14 or 15. Start the claret silk down the hook shank and tie in two dark rusty-dun cock hackle points for the wings, 1. Continue the silk in close even turns down the shank, 2, to the bend and there tie in three dun cock hackle fibres, 3, followed by a length of fine gold wire, 4. Now fasten in place a length of condor herl dyed brownish-red, 5.

Wind the condor herl to form a neatly tapered body and rib in close even turns with the gold wire, 6. Secure all and remove the waste. Take the wings and lift into an upright position and spread into a "V", securing with turns of silk, 7. It helps at this stage to put a very tiny drop of varnish at the wing roots.

Tie in a light-greenish-olive cock hackle, 8, and a brown-olive hackle, 9. Wind together both behind and in front of the wings, 10. Finish the fly with a neatly tapered head, and varnish.

Grey Fox Variant

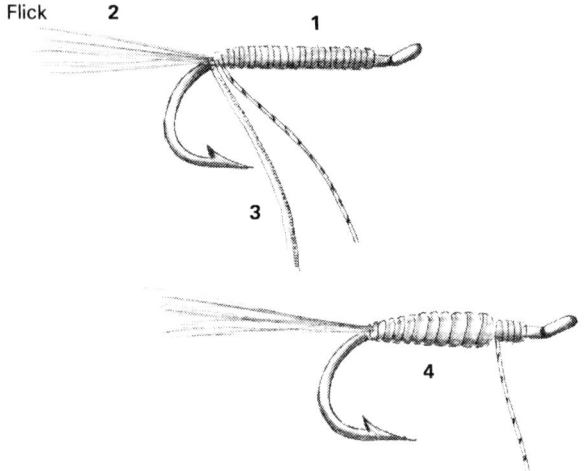

The United States has produced many first class fly tyers and one of the best is a man called Art Flick. Born in 1904 in New York he knew little of angling, other than dangling a worm off the end of the pier, until his parents moved to the Catskill Mountain area of New York State when he was 15 years old. His interest in trout fishing was quickly aroused. At the age of 17 he took a job in Kingston, where flowed the famous Esopus river, and he spent much time fishing the wet fly. A friendly circuit judge showed him what dry fly fishing was all about and from then on he was a committed dry-fly man.

In 1934 he moved from Kingston to West Kill where he was within easy reach of two other famous trout waters, the Westkill and the Schorarie, though still only eight miles from his first love, the Esopus. Shortly after his move he became friendly with Preston Jennings, author of *A Book of Trout Flies*, 1935, and it was Jennings who encouraged Flick to dress dry flies.

Apart from his fly-tying skills, Flick will always be remembered for his classic book *A Streamside Guide*, published first in 1947, and which ran to six editions, plus reprints. The book gives a highly detailed record of the natural flies and their imitation for use on his local waters. He collected and examined the natural insects almost every

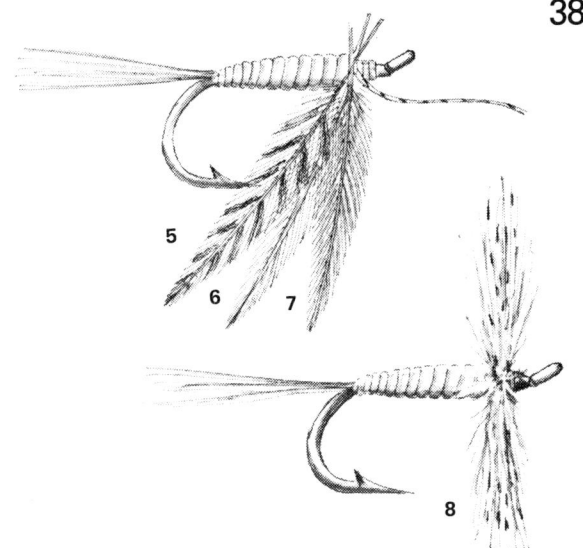

day for three years before he put pen to paper.

Flick's fly-tying reputation went from strength to strength and his patterns were in great demand. If he had a personal favourite style of fly it was the variant. Here his views agreed with those of our own William Baigent, who pioneered the very long hackle style of dressing. Like Baigent he considered that the play of the long fibres on the surface stimulated the trout in some manner. Flick's Grey Fox Variant dressed so has long been a favourite with American anglers. Such a successful fly deserves to be much better known on our own streams. I hope this will stimulate you to experiment with the variant style.

The hook size in the States is generally 10 or 12, but I suggest you use a 14 over here. Wind the primrose silk, 1, to the bend of the hook in close even turns and there tie in tail whisks of ginger cock hackle fibres, 2, followed by a light ginger or cream coloured stripped cock hackle stalk, 3. Wind the silk forward, followed by the hackle stalk in neat close turns to stimulate the segmented body, 4. Secure and remove waste. Now tie in three hackles, a grizzly cock, 5, a light ginger, 6, and a dark ginger, 7. They all have one thing in common—very long fibres. Wind the three hackles to form a dense close band, 8. Complete with a varnished whip-finished head.

Super Grizzly

Goddard

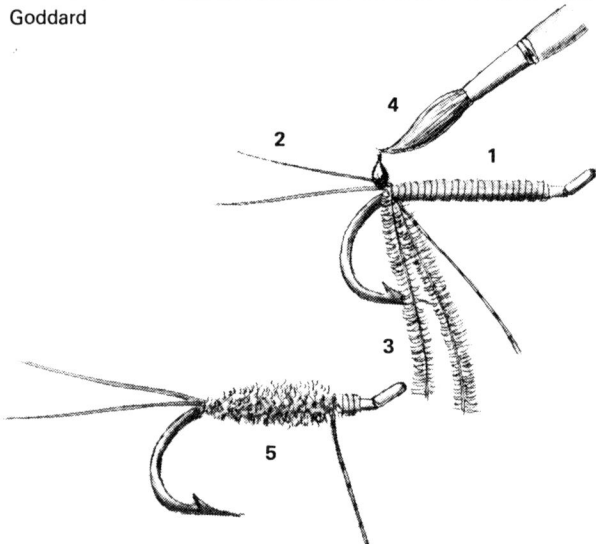

A new pattern devised by John Goddard is always an event worth noting, for experience has shown me that he does not produce new dressings willy nilly. Each is the result of careful thought, research and testing over many months before he is prepared to put his name to a fly that really does catch trout.

Such a fly is the Super Grizzly. In fact, at the time of writing the book, the fly is still on the "secret list" and I have given John my word that the pattern will not be disclosed to anyone until you see it in print. Goddard is too long in the tooth to wax enthusiastic over any old flash-in-the-pan pattern, but in this case he writes to me of "astonishing success" with the Super Grizzly over the past two years on southern chalk streams. This fly, and quite a few others, will be featured in a new book that is the joint work of Goddard and Brian Clarke, author of that best seller *The Pursuit of Stillwater Trout*, 1975. The combination of Goddard and Clarke provides a doughty measure of fly fishing, fly tying and entomological experience and I look forward to their new book with impatience.

The Super Grizzly was originally developed for fishing the Kennet where, on certain beats, the conditions dictate a

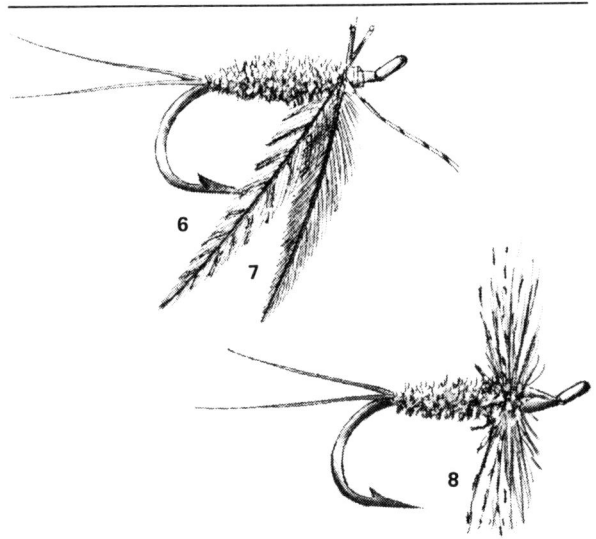

well-hackled fly to ensure flotation. It is a general pattern and can be fished throughout the season. The fly is interesting because of the tail fibres. Goddard had long been dissatisfied with the usual cock hackle fibres and cast his net around for a more durable alternative. He opted for muskrat or mink whiskers—not the most easily obtainable material. He does suggest an alternative—fine horse hair. He is also of the firm opinion that the muskrat or mink provides a far more pleasing silhouette when viewed from below; also they are extremely durable.

The hook size is either 14 or 16 fine wire hooks. Wind the hot-orange tying silk in close even turns, 1, down the hook shank and at the bend tie in two muskrat or mink whiskers, 2. Now tie in three natural heron herls, 3, which will form the body. Take a drop of varnish on a dubbing needle point and place it between the tail fibres, 4, holding them out in a "V" formation. Now twist together the heron herls and wind around the hook shank to form the body, 5. Secure and remove the waste ends. Tie in a good quality grizzle hackle, 6, and a natural red cock hackle, 7, back to back. Wind together to form a dense hackle, 8. Complete the fly with a whip-finished head and then varnish.

Barton Bug

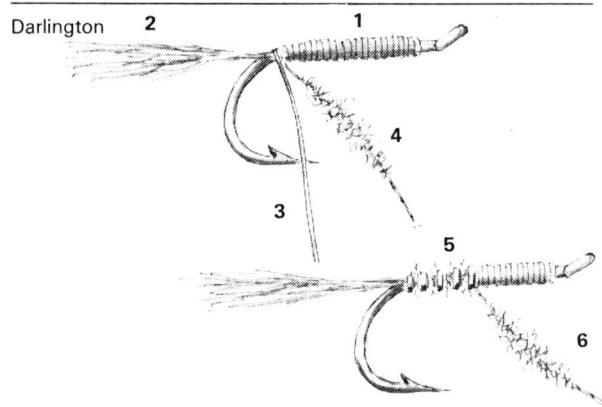

Darlington

I have a distinct problem with this fly for I am not sure if one should describe it as a nymph that floats or as a dry fly that sinks. I had better qualify this. In 1970 Roy Darlington fished with regularity the upper reaches of the River Itchen where the brown trout can be mighty selective. In many instances the trout appeared to be rising to floating medium olives and yet the usual patterns were totally ignored, though in fact so were the natural duns. The obvious assumption was that the trout were taking nymphs just below the surface film, but Skues' excellent nymph patterns were also ignored.

The following winter Darlington sat and thought about the problem and devised an emergent pattern with the following criteria in mind: (a) the pattern should be supported by the hackle in front; (b) the tails should be below the surface; (c) the tails should be exaggerated in imitate the shuck. To devise such a pattern that would float every time at the front end, while the rear of the fly was submerged, was not easy. He experimented with deer hair, small pieces of shaped polystyrene and similar materials, but after much trial and error he hit upon the right dressing which has been highly successful. It would be as well to detail the tying before describing the method of fishing the Barton Bug.

The hook can vary between 12 and 14. The primrose tying silk, 1, is taken in close even turns down to the bend and there a bunch of long rabbit fur fibres, from the back of a rabbit, are tied in, 2, followed by a length of fine gold wire,

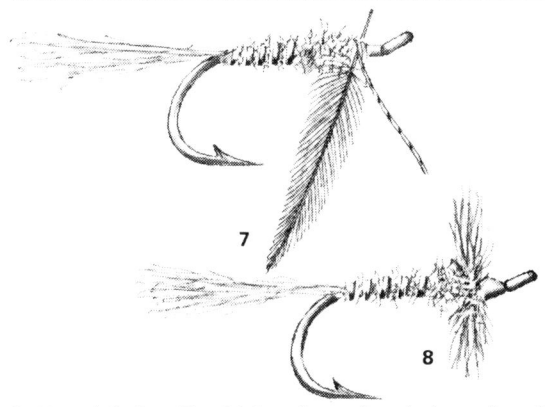

40

3. Now dub the silk with hare's ear fur, 4, dressed on thinly for the body area. Wind the body and rib with the wire, 5. Remove the waste wire. Dub the silk once more, being more generous with the hare's fur, so that a pronounced thorax shape is made when wound round the hook, 6. Tie in an absolutely top quality short-fibred blue dun cock hackle, 7, and wind in the usual manner, 8. Finish off with the usual whip finish.

Now to the fishing. When the trout are taking the emergent fly—that difficult half way stage between nymph and dun—soak the hackle of the fly in some good quality floatant and thoroughly wet the tails with saliva, or, if you are fastidious, any gin or scotch you may have to hand! The plot now becomes obvious, half floating and half sinking. In May 1971 the pattern had its first trial on the Itchen when medium olives started to hatch out. Darlington observed that in ten rises only an average of two duns were taken. The Barton Bug was tied on and within a distance of 150 yards three brace of trout were taken, the best being just under the two-pound mark.

Roy Darlington tells me that subsequent years on the Itchen, particularly after 1974 when he took over the famed Abbots Barton water and had ample opportunity to fish, the Barton Bug has proved to be a real "nailer". My only concern is what G. E. M Skues would have said to have a fly so named floating on his hallowed beats.

Terry's Terror

Terry

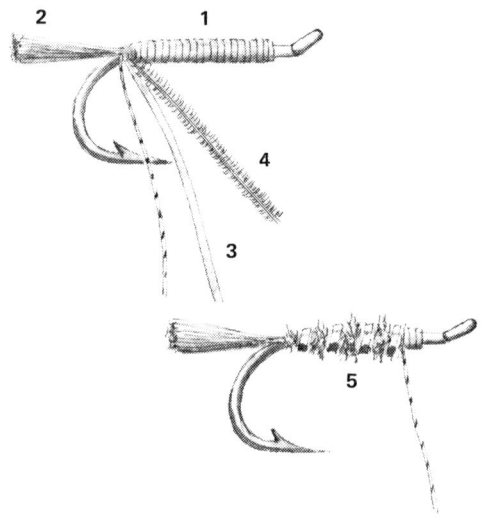

Another dry fly that carries the seal of approval of that knowledgable fly fisher and professional fly tyer, Peter Deane of Eastbourne. In fact, Deane goes so far as to state that the Terry's Terror is the best all-round dry fly pattern for any stream or river he has come upon since first starting to tie flies in 1948. That is praise indeed.

The original Terry's Terror was suggested by the late Dr. Cecil Terry who lived in Bath, and it was taken up by the late Ernest Lock, a well known fly tyer who operated in Andover. Ernest Lock was the son of John Lock, the inventor of Lock's Fancy, a chalkstream pattern that found great favour in the early years of this century. For a period of his life John Lock was a keeper on the Itchen at Kingsworthy when Halford had a rod on that particular water, and he gained a good reputation for highly durable flies that cocked beautifully on the water. His son, Ernest, was his equal in style and quality. Together, he and Terry popularised this pattern and it became a firm favourite of countless anglers.

I am pleased to have the opportunity to bring this pattern to a wider audience, because since my original cor-

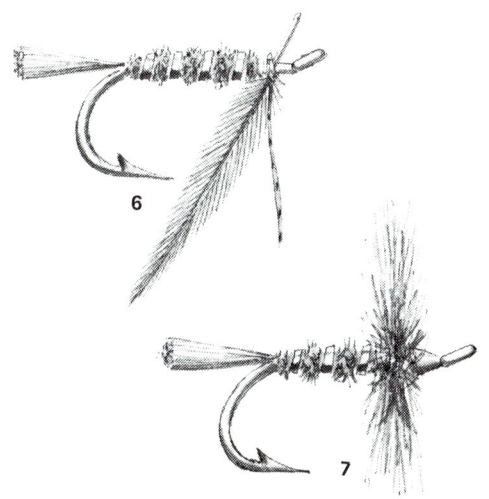

respondence in 1972 with Peter Deane I have used this pattern on many rivers. While I have not found it to be the magic touchstone to take all trout (was there ever such a fly) I have to agree with Peter Deane that it is a topping all-rounder, representing all the stages of the olive's from hatching nymph to spinner. Dressed very small, it is frequently taken when the iron blue is about, and on large hooks it has been known to do duty as a sedge.

To tie the fly place in the vice a hook ranging from 16 to 12 and carefully wind the tying silk, 1, down the hook shank to the bend. There tie in a tag of equal parts of orange and yellow dyed goat hair, cut short and flared, 2. Follow this with a length of flat copper tinsel, 3, and a single strand of peacock herl, 4.

Wind the peacock herl to form the body and rib with the flat copper tinsel, 5. Tie in a good quality fox-red cock hackle, 6, and turn in the usual manner, 7. Complete with a whip-finished head. The bottom half of the hackle was trimmed with scissors on the original fly, but I have not found this adds to the attraction of the pattern.

Assassine

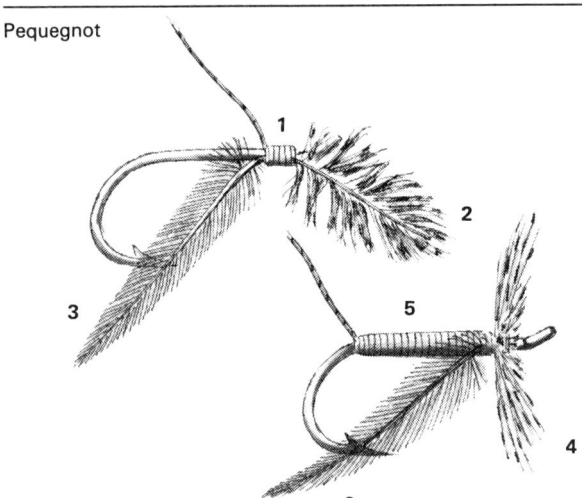

Not often do we find a French dry fly in a British angling book. In fact, it would almost seem that fly fishers on this side of the Channel do not realise the French have equally good streams and rivers, including chalkstreams. I recall the late Oliver Kite waxing lyrical about such fishing and each year he used to go to cast a fly on those waters.

Dr. J. P. Pequegnot, author of *L'Art de la Pêche à la Mouche Sèche*, a book highly respected in his own country, wrote to me some years ago and gave me the dressing of one of his own patterns I have found very successful on our waters. Pequegnot states quite firmly that the pattern does not represent a particular insect or group of insects, rather it is an abstract pattern devised to give maximum flotation. He is also quite convinced that a well-marked partridge hackle has a distinct attraction for the trout. Certainly many French patterns specify the use of a partridge hackle, and have done for countless years.

First tied in 1964, the Assassine is one of Pequegnot's most used flies, and he certainly gets his fair share of trout. He very kindly sent to me examples of his fly and they did prove to be extremely good floaters and, more to the point, attractive to the trout. The method of tying I found most interesting and I do feel that it has much to recommend it in

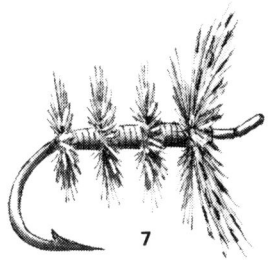

this day and age when top quality hackles are becoming more and more difficult to find. Let me show you what I mean by going through the stages of tying the Assassine.

The hook size can range from 12 to 15. Having placed your hook in the vice start the yellow, or olive, waxed tying silk down the shank, 1, and tie in a grey or brown well-mottled partridge hackle, 2, concave side to the front. Tie in a smokey-grey cock hackle, 3. Now wind the partridge hackle back to the grey hackle and secure, removing the waste end, 4. Take two or three turns of silk hard up against the partridge feather and force the fibres forward.

Continue the silk in close even turns to the bend of the hook, 5. Now wind the smokey-grey hackle, 6, hard up behind the partridge feather for two turns and then palmer down the shank in open turns to the bend, 7, tying off at the bend and removing the waste hackle stalk and silk.

Pequegnot is quick to admit he did not invent the method of tying, the French firm of Ragot having tied flies in this manner for many years. Certainly it is a style which has considerable scope for development, being ideal for forcing hackle fibres into a forward position and thereby giving them added support and rigidity.

Devon Dumpling

Nice

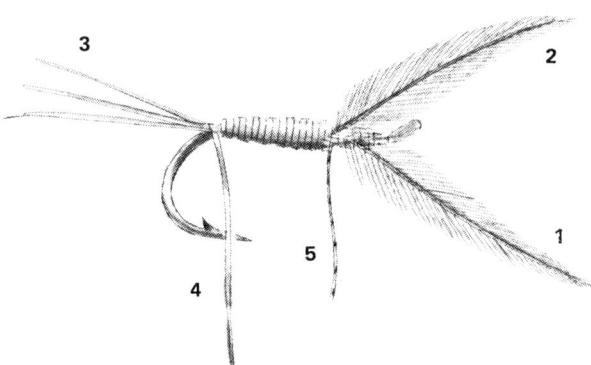

Another pattern from that highly competent fly tyer in Sidmouth, Devon, James Nice. Generally unknown outside the waters of that particular area, this fly is worth a much wider audience and I now present it with every confidence. Fished correctly, it has proved to be one of the best flies in my box. No doubt the palmer style of dressing is a great help to flotation and I wonder why we do not see more of it. I'm convinced trout do not count a fly's legs.

The reasoning behind the fly was that Nice required a dressing that would bounce along the tumbling waters usually found at the head of pools on fast rivers. The two hackles ensure that it really does float well and I find it the ideal fly for what I call "bouncy water". The old Derbyshire tyers of the Bumble's knew a thing or two.

Because of Nice's insistence on his particular tying method—and not wishing to have an hour's wigging on the telehone—I have illustrated the method in accordance with his instructions. As drawn, the fly is tied as it was in 1942, the year of its inception. After the introduction of D. F. M., Nice has tied this pattern with a body of orange or lime fluorescent silk. Old red-necked reactionary that I am, I prefer the silk-bodied version.

The hook size is 14 for rivers and 12 for stillwaters. Start the yellow tying silk down the hook shank for twelve turns and tie in sharp bright natural blue-dun cock hackle, 1.

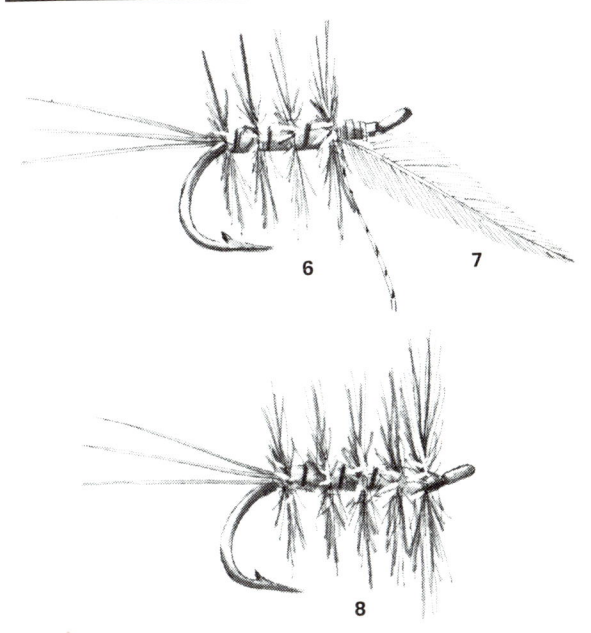

43

Wind for a further two turns and tie in the body hackle, 2, which is another blue-dun. Continue the tying silk turns, trapping in the hackle stalks, and half way to the bend cut off the stalks, then continue the silk to the bend. There tie in cock hackle fibres from a blue-dun, 3. At the same time tie in the ribbing wire of the finest gold or silver wire, 4. Return the tying silk in close even turns up the shank to within one turn of the body hackle, 5.

Wind the body hackle towards the bend in wide turns. Retain tension on the hackle while you work the ribbing wire through the hackle to secure it, 6, in front of the first turn. Remove the waste wire and wind the tying silk forward to within four turns of the original starting point.

Now wind the head tackle, 7, forward up to the tying silk and secure, removing waste end of hackle, 8. One more turn to catch in the snippet ends then whip finish back four turns prior to varnishing the head. A fly tied thus should never come untied!

Driffield Dun

Origin unknown

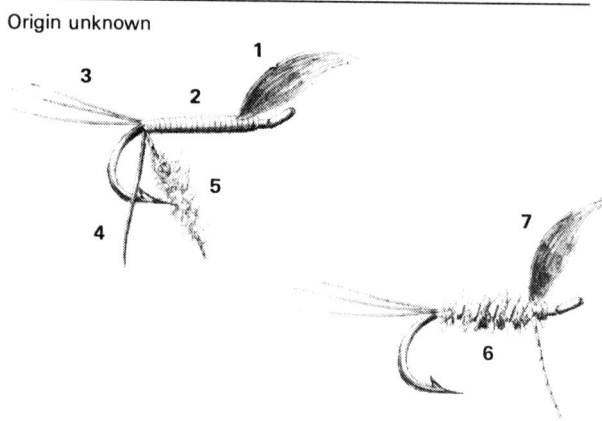

I am on solid ground with this pattern for I was born at Driffield, East Yorkshire some — never mind how many — years ago almost within casting distance of the celebrated Driffield Beck. As a boy I used to watch with interest, tinged with envy, those fly fishers who wandered the banks, little knowing that one day I too would have the good fortune to be a member of that ancient angling brotherhood, and that I would tread in the footsteps of those old boys, now long gone.

One's roots always pull at the heartstrings and after many years of living away from the Yorkshire Wolds I have succumbed, much to the consternation of my bank manager, and now own what my wife calls our "bolt hole", where we can escape from the rush of the Midlands to the peace and quiet of Driffield. A small place situated between the stream and the pub . . . bliss.

Despite being a native of Driffield, I have yet to discover who first tied this fly and who named it. The first writer of note to comment on the Driffield chalkstream was Alexander Mackintosh, who in 1806 wrote that literary gem *The Driffield Angler*. A fly tyer of some imagination, it is quite obvious that most of his patterns were evolved from a study of the natural insect and not from other men's dressings, and yet a close examination of his work shows no pattern remotely resembling the Driffield Dun.

Courtney Williams in *A Dictionary of Trout Flies* sug-

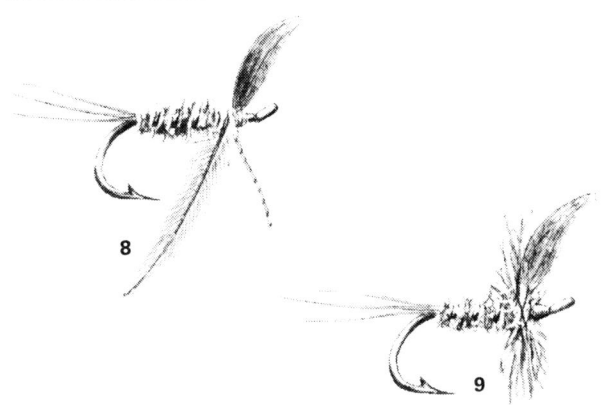

gests that the fly is of the spider type. For once the oracle was way off beam for it is not, and never has been, a spider pattern. The first reference to the Driffield Dun I can find is in an article by "Sarcelle" in the spring issue of the Flyfishers' Club Journal of 1922, where he writes of "the traditional pattern of the Driffield Dun", putting forward the view that it was a local variant of the Whirling Blue Dun. Again I cannot agree, for the body material is very different. That the fly was created on my own doorstep and I cannot trace its origins, is doubly infuriating. I would welcome the help of any reader who has more information.

Now to the fly. The hook size is usually 14, though it works very well on a 16. Start the grey tying silk down the hook shank and tie in two slips of pale starling wing feather fibre, 1. Continue the silk down to the bend in close even turns, 2, and tie in the whisks of pale ginger cock hackle fibres, 3, followed by a length of unwaxed yellow silk, 4. Dub the tying silk sparingly with lead-coloured rabbit's fur, 5, and wind up the shank to form the body, followed by close turns of the ribbing silk, 6. Bring the wings to a more slightly upright position, though still maintaining a positive forward slant, and secure with figure-of-eight turns of silk, 7. Tie in a sharp ginger cock hackle, 8, and wind on in the usual manner, 9. Complete the fly with a neatly whip-finished head and carefully varnish.

Tup's Indispensable

Austin

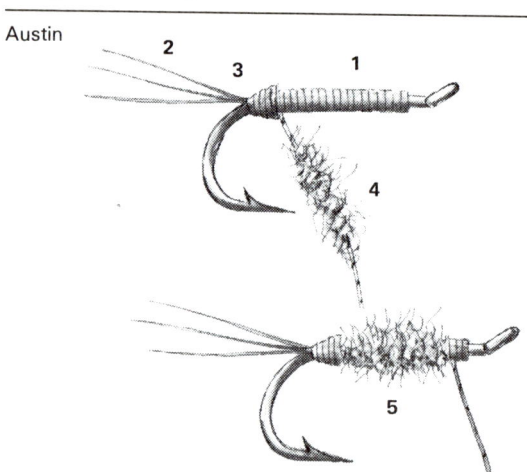

This fly is surely one of the best known in the dry fly fishers' armoury. Devised in 1900 by R. A. Austin, a most competent fly tyer who lived in Devon, it was brought to general prominence by G. E. M. Skues, who was in regular correspondence with Austin. In 1900 Austin sent Skues a pattern of the then un-named fly seeking the latter's opinion. Skues replied, requesting details of the rather odd body material. Austin sent him a small bag of the dubbing, explaining that it was a mixture of wool taken from the scrotum of a tup (ram), which no doubt accounted for the yellowish tinge caused by the urine, to which was added a pinch of lemon hair from a spaniel, and seasoned with a small amount of fur from the poll of a hare, plus a little red mohair to turn the witch's brew a slightly pinkish shade.

Skues carried out a series of successful experiments with this pattern and after some while suggested that the red mohair be discarded in favour of red seal's fur, surely Skues' favourite body material. That Austin agreed to the change is evident from subsequent letters. He also agreed to Skues christening the fly the Tup's Indispensable.

So highly did Austin value the make-up of the body dubbing, he asked Skues to keep it a secret until after he, Austin, was dead. When he did die in 1911 his daughter carried on the fly-tying business, the demand being mainly for

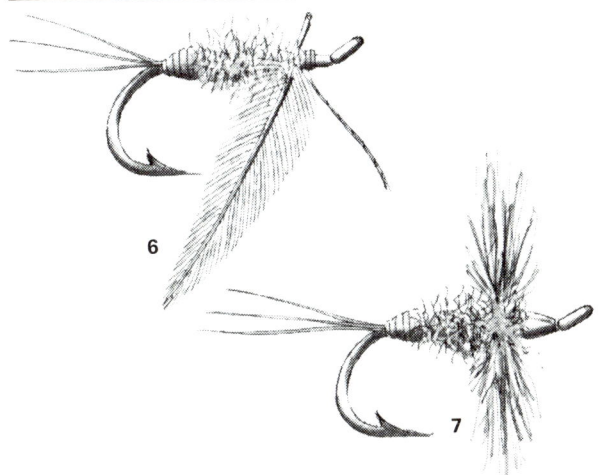

the Tup's Indispensable, and so to protect her interests and exclusivity Skues kept the secret of the dubbing until her retirement in the early nineteen-thirties, and it only became known via the Flyfishers' Club Journal in 1934. It almost seems that Austin created a monster, for in a letter to Skues he confided that he was sick to death of tying the thing, and that the River Frome stank of Tup's Indispensables from Maiden Newton down to the sea!

Despite the dubbing material having been common knowledge since 1934, it is truly amazing what horrors are passed off to the angling public as Tup's. I have seen examples in tackle shops with bodies ranging from shocking pink to daffodil yellow. For such bastardisation there is no excuse. If this book does nothing else, I hope it provides for more accurate examples.

The hook size is generally 14 or 16. Wind the yellow tying silk in close even turns down the hook shank, 1, to the bend and there tie in the tail whisks, 2, of lightish blue cock hackle fibres. Take the silk back up the shank for three or four turns, 3, and then dub the silk with the described mixture, 4. Wind the dubbed silk to form the body, 5.

Tie in a good light blue cock hackle, 6, ideally with yellow spangle flecks, and then wind in the usual way, 7. Complete with a varnished whip finish.

Itchen Olive

Mackie

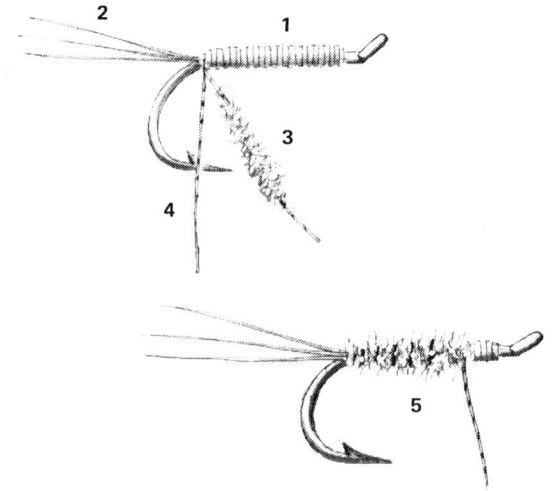

During my visits to the Winchester area, and in particular
the Abbots Barton beats of the River Itchen, it has been my
distinct pleasure to meet and talk with Gordon Mackie, a
fisherman of considerable ability and a most keen observer
of the way of trout with the natural fly. His periodic articles
in the angling press confirm that he is very observant and a
man worth noting.

His pattern, which he calls, simply, the Itchen Olive, was
devised to represent a range of what he refers to as "the
pale stuff"; small spurwings, pale evening duns, etc.,
naturals that are often quite prolific on the banks of that
lovely river. After quite a few seasons on trial this pattern
has now become his top favourite and he uses it on all
waters and at all times of the year.

The fly also has the great advantage of being easily tied
by the novice fly dresser. It is also quite an easy matter to
change the overall hue of the body by simply ringing the
changes with the tying silk, right through from primrose to
dark brown. Fly tyers who have not yet realised the subtle
body colour changes that can be effected would do well to
experiment with silk colours. The old-time wet fly tyers
certainly knew a thing of two when they sparsely dubbed

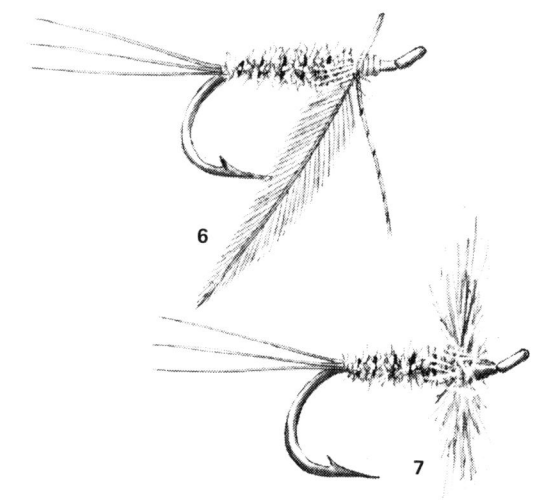

their tying silks, allowing the colour of the silk to filter through the dubbing material. Such dressings can be highly attractive to both the trout and the tyer.

I fully intend to give this pattern a thorough testing over the coming seasons. Only time will tell if it works as well for me as for Gordon Mackie, though I suspect from the cut of its jib it will join that select band of patterns always in my fly-box.

As previously mentioned the tying is quite simple. The hook size is generally number 14. Wind the primrose tying silk in close even turns down the hook shank, 1, to the bend and there tie in five or six top quality light grey cock hackle fibres, 2. Now tie in a separate length of silk for the ribbing, 4, followed by waxing the original tying silk and bubing with medium-grey seal's fur, not too dark, 3. Carefully wind a sparse body and rib it with the separate tying silk, 5. Secure the rib and remove the waste dubbing.

Tie in a good quality light-grey cock hackle, 6, and wind three or four turns only round the hook shank, 7. Remove the waste hackle, whip finish the head and carefully varnish. The fly should be lightly tied so that it floats high on the surface.

Wickham's Fancy

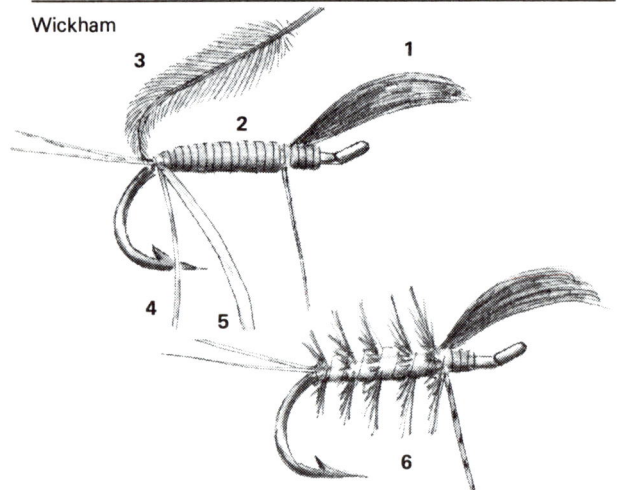

Wickham

Another great dry fly from the vintage era of the Hampshire chalkstreams that has found its way to less exalted waters as the years have gone by, though without losing its trout-taking capability. A fly that makes no pretentions to having an original counterpart, though I tend to agree with Courtney Williams that it serves very well as a sedge.

My reason for the fly's inclusion in this book is because it was the favourite pattern of an old river keeper I knew well many years ago, a gentleman who caught more trout than most of us will ever see and who used only three flies, dry flies that is, the Wickham's Fancy being top of his list. I used to say that I would write an article about him and his Wickhams but the reply was always the same: "Nay lad, wait till ah've gan on or else iverybody will be wantin' me te dress em Wickhams and me ees aint what tha wor".

But to the history of the fly. It is generally accepted that it was suggested by Dr. T. C. Wickham, and first tied by John Hammond of Winchester. I must admit to nagging doubts about the first man to tie it, for I believe there is a good case to be made for George Holland as the first tyer. To my knowledge Hammond operated from 1856 to 1880 and I think the fly was devised after 1880, putting it into the Holland bracket of 1885 to 1896. Space does not allow a full investigation here, but the matter is worth looking into

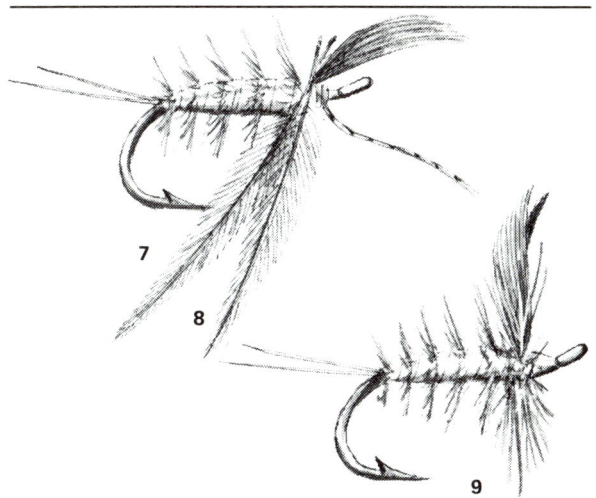

if you have the inclination and the time.

Courtney Williams also put forward another contender as the originator, a Capt. John Wickham, with yet another fly tyer as the first man to dress them, George Currell of Winchester, and gives a date of 1884. G. E. M. Skues often referred to Dr. Wickham, as the inventor of the fly and I chose to believe Skues in so far as he knew the man.

The tying is a little complicated but worth the effort. Hook size is generally 14 or 16. Start the brown tying silk down the hook shank and tie in two slips of medium starling, 1. Continue the silk down the shank, 2, and at the bend tie in a ginger-red cock hackle, 3, and tail whisks of gallina feather fibre dyed brownish-red. Follow these with a length of fine gold wire, 4, and a length of flat gold tinsel, 5. Wind the silk back up to the wings. Now wind the flat gold tinsel over and secure.

At this stage you may care to coat the tinsel with clear varnish. Wind the hackle in wide turns and secure with the following turns of the gold wire rib. The body is now as fig. 6. Bring the wings into an upright position and tie in two ginger cock hackles, 7 and 8. Wind the hackles behind and in front of the wings, 9, and complete with a varnished whip finished head. I would add that the fly seems equally effective without the wing.

Mistigri

Pequegnot

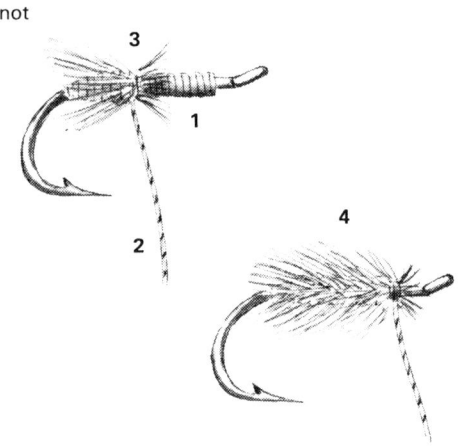

A further excellent French dry fly from the tying vice of Dr. J. P. Pequegnot of Besançon, the man who, back in 1972, gave me the very interesting Assassine dressing described earlier in this book.

Pequegnot's Mistigri was evolved following a number of fishing trips to the River Doubs near Goumis, where the trout seemed to be feeding exclusively on small black stoneflies, an insect that is very prolific in the Jura region during the early spring.

Dr. Pequegnot had never been totally satisfied with the usual stonefly dressings and his frustrating days on the Doubs caused him to sit down and re-think the matter from the fly-tyers' point of view. He reported to me that his new dressing was very well received by the trout and that down the years he has had no cause to tie any other. Like the Assassine, the pattern shows a refreshing approach in fly tying technique, and it is worth spending time on the method so that all is made clear.

The hook size is usually between 14 and 16. Take the black tying silk, 1, in close even turns down the hook shank to the bend and return, again with close even turns, to point 2. Now we come to a more complicated operation. Take a small bunch of black hackle fibres, interspersed with a few brown partridge feather fibres, and spin round the hook shank by taking a turn of silk and pulling tight, 3.

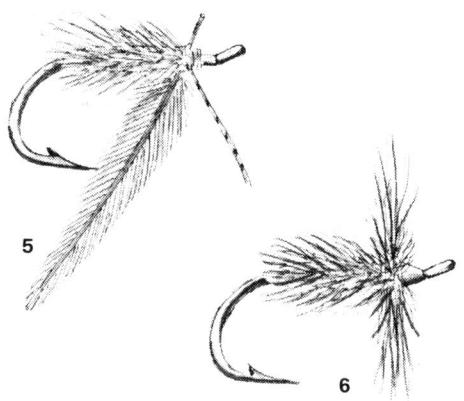

48

It is really easier to do than to describe. Those of you who tie Muddler Minnows, using deer hair, will be familiar with the technique. Continue to build up the body by placing further bunches of hackle fibres along the hook shank, 4. Where the body ends tie in a good quality black cock hackle, 5, and wind very close to the body hackles, no more than two turns, 6. Complete the fly with a whip-finished and varnished head.

Pequegnot's original dressing had a body of peacock herl, but experience has shown him that such is not really required. Its deletion certainly makes for faster tying. The important point is to make the body hackle fibres stand out at approx. 20 to 25 degrees from the shank. Given a good soaking in floatant, this fly bounces along in a most perky manner.

Though the pattern described is of a sombre hue, one can ring the changes in hackle colour to imitate many species of stoneflies. Pequegnot wrote and told me that when fishing a chalkstream where the trout were feeding on pale wateries he presented out of curiosity, a small Mistigri. He had more trout to the stonefly than to his representation of the pale watery! Make of that what you will. Tied on very small hooks, I can thoroughly recommend this fly, when black gnats are about.

Hassam's Pet

Hassam

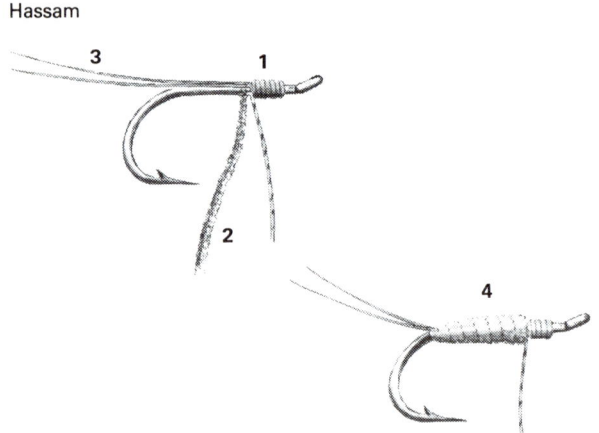

We are now coming to the end of the book and I intend to indulge myself by including a dry fly devised by the man G. E. M. Skues admired above all other tyers of the fly: C. A. Hassam. I have seen a fly tied by this man and for absolute delicacy it would take some beating. Unfortunately I do not have an example in my collection and so if any reader . . . ?

For many years Hassam lived and fished in Derbyshire, the rivers Wye and Derwent being his regular haunts. Skues, in his book *Sidelines, Sidelights and Reflections*, points out that the rather unusual winging style of Hassam bears great similarity to that of James Ogden, the author of *Ogden On Fly Tying*, 1879, who was also of Derbyshire extraction, and Skues poses the question: was there some common local origin for this method? In the Summer 1929 issue of the Flyfishers' Club Journal Skues set down in great detail every stage in the tying of a Hassam dry fly, all two and a half pages of it!

Space within this book does not allow such a full description and so I have described the tying in a simplified form that can be easily tied by a newcomer to the craft. Nevertheless the materials are correct and I can vouch for the fact that such a tie was a favourite of Hassam. It does noble work when the small olives are about. The body material when well soaked in floatant turns a most attractive pale

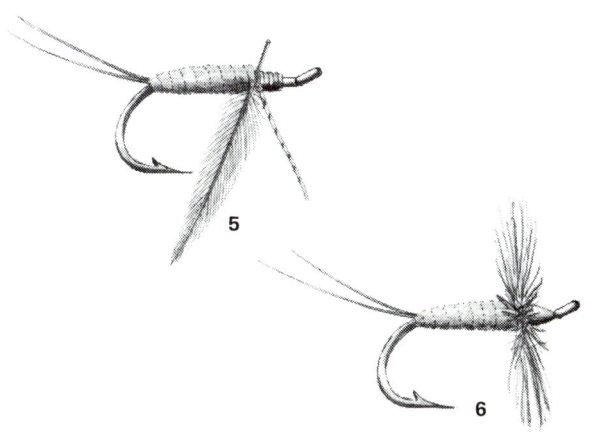

green. An angler on the Itchen is reported to have had three brace of trout on this pattern before lunchtime, the best weighing 3 lbs and 2 ¾ lbs. I, too, have taken very good fish on Hassam's Pet from such diverse waters as a Test carrier, the Driffield stream, Foston, the Yorkshire Derwent and the Northumberland Coquet.

A word of warning in the dressing of the body. You will note that the tying silk is not taken all the way along the hook shank and that the tail whisks must be tied in with the first turns of silk, therefore they must be quite long. Remember that floss does not have the "biting" power of silk and if secured with the floss only they have a very good chance of pulling out.

Place the hook, usually a number 16, in the vice and wind the primrose tying silk, 1, down the shank for five or six turns only. Its only purpose is to provide a bed for the hackle. Tie in a length of pale yellow floss, 2, and tail whisks of pale ginger cock hackle fibres, 3. Take the floss and wind in close even turns down the shank and over the whisks. At the bend pass one turn of the floss under the whisks and return up the shank to form the body, 4. Tie in a very pale ginger cock hackle of top quality, 5, and wind over the silk bed in the usual manner, 6. Complete with a varnished whip-finished head.

Merry Widow

Elphick

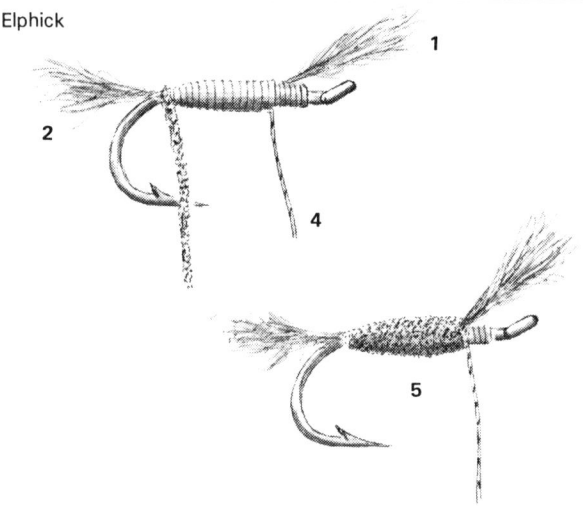

Finally we come to a pattern designed by a lady fly tyer who is equally skilled in the taking of trout, sea-trout and salmon as she is in manipulating fur and feather. Down the years the ladies have always been well to the fore in fly tying, possibly more so in days past than today. At the turn of the century such towns as Redditch must have been knee deep in hackles, as the girls, both in factory and at home, twirled feathers to create flies by the million. Of course, the majority of them were simply duplicating existing patterns and would not have recognised a natural olive if it had settled upon their noses.

Today far fewer girls are so employed, but those that do take to the craft of tying are highly knowledgable and skillful, and most inventive. Three modern lady fly dressers spring to mind: Jackie Wakeford, Megan Boyd (surely the queen of salmon fly tyers) and Brenda Elphick. It is a fly by the last named that we now examine.

Brenda Elphick was trained by Peter Deane and her natural aptitude for the craft quickly made her a permenent member of his company. Deane is quick to recognise talent and he believes that Brenda Elphick is the best professional all-round fly tyer in the country today. Having examined her work in detail I would not dispute that comment. It is

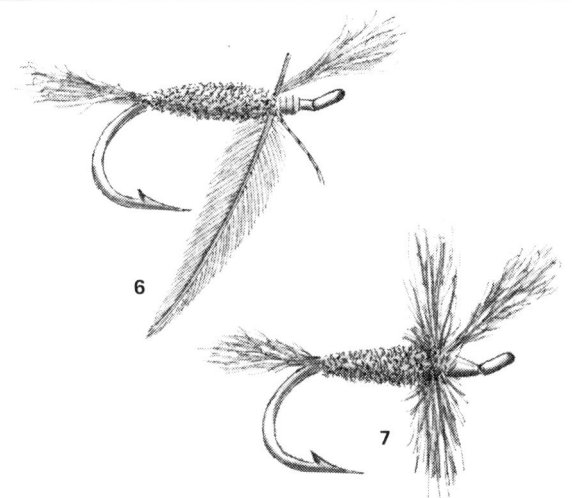

quite easy for the skilled amateur to tie one fly to perfection, but quite another matter to reproduce that style and quality over two dozen flies of the same type—to reproduce them so that one fly is indistinguishable from the next. I often think that fly-tying competitions should be so arranged, for a good tyer must be a consistent tyer.

The Merry Widow was based upon the Wulff series popularised in this country by Peter Deane, and it was devised some eight or nine years ago by Brenda Elphick, since when it has become a firm favourite among Deane's customers who fish stillwaters, especially on hot, still days.

The original dressing had a body of black rabbit's fur, but as the material is not all that readily available, black floss was substituted and worked every bit as well. Place the hook, sizes between 16 and 10, in the vice and start the black tying silk down the shank, tying in a wing of black dyed calf tail fibres, 1. Continue the silk down the shank to the bend and tie in a few fibres of the same calf hair, 2, also a length of black floss, 3. Return the silk to point 4. Wind the floss to form a neatly-tapered body, 5. Tie in a black cock hackle, 6, and wind behind the wing, 7. It is essential that the wing has a positive forward slant and is not split. Complete the fly with a whip finished and varnished head.

Index